CAREER NETWORKING

How To Books on jobs and careers

Career Networking
Career Planning for Women
Finding a Job in Canada
Finding a Job in Computers
Finding a Job in New Zealand
Finding a Job with a Future
Getting a Job after University
Getting Your First Job
How to Apply for a Job
How to Be a Freelance Journalist
How to Be a Freelance Sales Agent
How to Be a Freelance Secretary
How to Become an Au Pair
How to Do Voluntary Work Abroad
How to Find Temporary Work
  Abroad
How to Get a Job Abroad
How to Get a Job in America
How to Get a Job in Australia
How to Get a Job in Europe
How to Get a Job in France
How to Get a Job in Germany
How to Get a Job in Hotels &
  Catering

How to Get a Job in Travel &
  Tourism
How to Get Into Radio
How to Get Into Films & Television
How to Know Your Rights at Work
How to Manage Your Career
How to Market Yourself
How to Return to Work
How to Start a New Career
How to Work from Home
How to Work in an Office
How to Work in Retail
How to Work with Dogs
How to Write a CV That Works
Living & Working in China
Surviving Redundancy
Working as a Holiday Rep
Working in Japan
Working on Contract Worldwide
Working on Cruise Ships
Working with Children
Working with Horses

Other titles in preparation

The How To Series now contains more than 200 titles in the following
  categories:

Business Basics
Family Reference
Jobs & Careers
Living & Working Abroad
Student Handbooks
Successful Writing

Please send for a free copy of the latest catalogue for full details (see back
cover for address).

JOBS & CAREERS

CAREER NETWORKING

How to develop the right contacts to
help you throughout your working life

Laurel Alexander

How To Books

Cartoons by Mike Flanagan

British Library Cataloguing in Publication Data
A catalogue record for this book is available from the British Library.

© Copyright 1997 by Laurel Alexander.

Published by How To Books Ltd, 3 Newtec Place, Magdalen Road,
Oxford OX4 1RE, United Kingdom.
Tel: (01865) 793806. Fax: (01865) 248780.

Note: The material contained in this book is set out in good faith for
general guidance and no liability can be accepted for loss or expense
incurred as a result of relying in particular circumstances on statements
made in the book. The laws and regulations are complex and liable to
change, and readers should check the current position with the relevant
authorities before making personal arrangements.

Produced for How To Books by Deer Park Productions.
Typeset by PDQ Typesetting, Stoke-on-Trent, Staffs.
Printed and bound by Cromwell Press, Broughton Gifford, Melksham,
Wiltshire.

Contents

Contents

List of Illustrations

Preface

If you are out of work, wanting promotion, wanting to be self-employed, coming back after a career break or seeking to break into management, you need to career network.

Networking is communication. Without communication, we remain in ignorance and miss out on opportunities for financial reward, improved status and exciting challenges. This book helps to de-mystify the term 'networking' and applies it to developing your career with confidence. By building self-esteem and assertive behaviour, you can make contact with all types of people who can help you develop your career potential.

Career networking is based on people skills. But this book also contains modern methods of networking such as using the Internet and being your own PR person. It will help you identify new ways to exploit your skills so that you will be seen as a specialist and thereby build a professional reputation with unlimited potential. Further information is provided on how to extend your network, starting your own network and get on other people's network.

I write this book as my way of networking with you, the reader, and I hope that you will pass on anything which you may learn and spread the networking web out even further.

Laurel Alexander

IS THIS YOU?

Employed   Returning to work

On promotion ladder

Making a career change   Training for work

Ambitious

Lacking self-confidence   Part-time worker

Working from home

Jobseeker   Self-employed

Planning your career

Networking for job leads   Retraining

Job applicant

Skilled   Professional

Wanting to become more assertive

Businessperson   Manager

Graduate

Been made redundant   Woman returner

Team member

Moving up to management   Specialist

Expert

Unemployed   Returning to study

1
Understanding Networking

DEFINING NETWORKING

This book is my way of making contact with you, the reader. I am sharing my ideas and experience, so that you can move forward in your career. We are both networking for work – myself as someone wanting the experience of research and writing and having the knowledge of career networking to share, and you as someone interested in developing their career through networking. Career networking is about:

- making contact with people

- developing that contact into a useful relationship

- gathering work-related information which is of use to you

- imparting work-related information which is of use to others

- giving and receiving mutual support

- staying in work

- developing work opportunities for the future.

Building bridges
We build bridges to get from one side of something to another. Using the techniques of networking, we can go from having a lack of skills to the acquisition of them, which in turn will move us forward in our career.

We can build bridges from one skill to another, from one rung of the career ladder up to the next, from one company to another, from one contact to another. The bridge is built on communication. How, what, when and to whom we communicate builds the bridge which gets us to from here to there.

Making contact
When we make contact with someone, we exchange energies, mental,

11

Using the fax	Writing letters
Getting on the Internet	Making a telephone call
Reading local and national press	Using E-mail
	Listening to the radio
Joining professional organisations	Watching TV
Attending meetings	Attending conferences
Joining Jobclubs	Joining support groups
Using employment agencies	Public library system
Visiting the pub	Attending a party
Answering an ad	Reading trade journals
Through your neighbours	Talking to relatives
Your doctor/dentist/optician	Your solicitor
Your accountant/bank manager	Local shopkeepers
Past college/university friends	Past school friends
Rotary Club colleagues	Past employers
Veterans associations	Club membership
Military organisations	Voluntary organisations
Previous clients	Previous/current tutors
Suppliers	Former work contacts
Friends	Freemasons
Your priest/rabbi/minister	Colleges/universities

Fig. 1. Ways in which you might network.

emotional or physical. Contacts are the life-line of the successful networker. Wherever they are: in the office, down the pub, sharing a meal with friends, attending a conference or seeing their accountant, a good networker is always making contact to see what's new.

Exchanging information
When we make contact, we inform people of what we are doing, and they tell us what they are up to. We ask each other questions and may help each other with answers. If you think of the last conversation you had with a friend, it was all about telling, asking, sharing, encouraging, challenging and inspiring each other. You were networking.

What you can get
Through exchanging information, career networking could give you support and increased opportunities to learn new skills, earn more money and have fresh challenges.

What you can give
Networking is a two-way operation. You have knowledge which other people could benefit from. You know someone who might help someone else. The more positive energy we can give out in helping others, the more we help ourselves.

Exercise: what is your existing network?

List all of the people with whom you have made personal, professional and domestic contact during the last week. Who has made contact with you? Look at Figure 1 for some ideas.

NETWORKING AS PART OF YOUR WORK STRATEGY

The world of work is changing fast and we need to develop the right skills to keep up with it. The skills necessary to find and win work are becoming almost as important as the job-specific skills themselves. More vacancies are filled through word of mouth and a speculative approach than any other method and the main skill necessary is that of networking.

What networking can do for your career

Gone are the days when we had a job straight from school and it lasted for as long as we wanted it to. Gone are the days of leaving one job in the morning and finding another six around the corner by mid-afternoon.

Many of us are still in the way of thinking that when we want a job, we look in the paper and there it is, waiting for us – and about sixty other people! The best way of getting work in this day and age is to network. To build up contacts wherever you go, to write a speculative letter to a company you think you would like to work for, to get yourself about, to let people know what you can do and that you are available to do it.

Networking puts us in control. Rather than waiting for people to come to us – which if we waited a month of Sundays, they may or may not do – we can be pro-active. We can take the initiative and get out there meeting people. Most of my work has come through networking although I didn't realise it at the time. Though using employment agencies, pushing myself forward, suggesting to potential employers where I might fit in, phoning people up and telling them I was available for work and using and developing my skills whenever I could so that I became a valuable asset, I became a successful networker.

Getting back to work

You may have just been made redundant. If you have been out of work for some time, it can become difficult to network. One reason is the withdrawal that can occur after being made redundant. Being out of work for a longer period of time can alter perception and cause a feeling of isolation. Clients have often said to me that their network of contacts has shrunk after being out of work for some time and this has led them into a loop of depression because of the loneliness, which in turn creates more apathy.

If you are claiming benefit, one effective way of beginning to network again is to join your local Jobclub. They offer support and advice on getting back to work including CV writing, sending out speculative letters, interview techniques and help with your jobsearch. They also help with the costs of postage.

You might also consider voluntary work as a way of networking.

You may not get paid for the contribution you make, but you might make a useful contact which could lead to paid work.

The promotion ladder

Networking is an ideal way to get promotion. Through getting yourself a mentor, being seen as a specialist and contributing to effectiveness and productivity, you might network yourself into a better paid and more fulfilling job.

Making a career change

You might fancy changing career altogether. By talking to friends, colleagues and professionals, you could get a new perspective on your working life. By networking with the local colleges and universities, you can find out the vocational training on offer to help you make that big step

Increasing your skills and knowledge

You may want to increase your skills-base, in which case, making yourself available for training would open up your horizons.

Improving your skills and knowledge occurs when you are pro-active. You might enrol on a training course, or ask someone at work to teach you, or you might teach yourself. Networking with people from whom you want to learn can improve your awareness of the learning opportunities available.

Assessing your career goals

In order to network with the right people, you need to know why you are networking. Take time to think about and answer the questions in the exercise below:

Exercise: assessing your career goals

- Do I want to return to work following a career break?
- Do I want to get any type of paid work I can following unemployment?
- Do I want to stay in the same line of work but with added responsibility?
- Do I want a different job with the same company?
- Do I want to make a career change?
- Do I want to work for myself?
- Do I want to return to education or training?

Action planning
When you have ascertained your objectives for career networking, you need to map out an action plan. Any action plan needs to be:

Specific	Wanting to network in order to develop management skills.
Measurable	When I can see my skills in action helping me to get promotion.
Achievable	I already use some management skills.
Realistic	Management is the next step up for me.
Time-bound	I want to be ready for my appraisal in six months' time.

DEVELOPING THE CONFIDENCE TO NETWORK

We need to have confidence in ourselves in order to network. Confidence is a state of mind which is reflected in our behaviour. When we experience a lack of confidence, we doubt our abilities, feel uncertain and indecisive. If this state of anxiety persists, we can hold ourselves back from taking risks or joining in activities. Confidence is self-respect, self-belief and a willingness to have a go, knowing you can cope with making a mistake.

When considering confidence, we need to:

- take responsibility for our personal power

- understand and accept that it is natural to feel apprehensive about opening ourselves up to others

- use the power of our intelligent mind to control our feelings.

Being confident doesn't mean that you will never feel doubtful again. It means that you can develop enough belief in yourself to sometimes feel vulnerable. Being confident means having enough belief in yourself, most of the time, to know that you can support yourself. No one can give us confidence. It grows within ourselves.

Claiming your power
Confidence is power – knowing that you have the choice and the power to deal with anything. We may believe that we don't have a right to determine what we want from life. There may be a belief

that to claim personal power is to be selfish. The truth is that we always have a choice and the more we learn to support ourselves, the more in charge of our lives we feel. We network in order to develop a support system which provides something we can hook into when we need additional information.

Positive thinking

Making choices means cultivating a positive mental attitude. In order to become more confident, we need to have belief in ourselves. We need to tell ourselves that we do have valuable skills and that our contributions can make a difference in the workplace. It is easy to cultivate a negative attitude without actually realising it.

A positive mental attitude indicates a belief system which is open to receiving the best that life can offer. Of course, life will occasionally dish up dirt, but a positive attitude will give rise to seeing problems as opportunities for challenge and growth. Confidence is the art of using our mental capabilities to overcome negative beliefs.

Developing a positive self-image

As we develop an inner understanding with ourselves, so we begin to present a different outer picture to the world. We present an image of confidence, openness and a genuine desire to connect with other people and new experiences. We stand taller with more pride in ourselves and hold our head up knowing we have a place in the world, as does everyone else. We smile more and maintain eye contact because we want to connect with others as we connect to ourselves. This means effective and productive career networking.

We take more chances because we know we can deal with success and failure. We define who we are to others and won't accept someone else's definition of us to suit themselves. We can ask for what we want and negotiate with others for a compromise. We are pro-active and initiate change in our lives.

Exercise: knowing yourself

Describe how you see yourself. Ask two other people, a man and a woman, how they see you.

Assertiveness at work

Having confidence in yourself is naturally linked to becoming an assertive person. To develop assertiveness means to develop a positive attitude about yourself, others and your place in the world and to demonstrate this through appropriate behaviours such as:

- being able to receive criticism without getting defensive
- being able to give constructive criticism
- being able to initiate relationships
- defining yourself to others
- making requests
- showing appreciation
- being persistent
- leading others
- being pro-active.

Networking can:

Gain you promotion	Establish objectives
Stimulate your mind	Increase your professionalism
Help get a career change	Increase your confidence
Make you new friends	Develop your visibility
Get you back to work	Assist your career planning
Expand your horizons	Make you more assertive
Help gain new skills	Be positive
Create opportunities	Help other people

Fig. 2. What networking can do for you.

BEING SEEN AS AN EXPERT

We all have something to sell. We may not have the professional qualifications, but we have the experience, knowledge and skills to peddle in the networking marketplace. If you are a keen gardener, you may belong to a gardening group which meets regularly – already you're networking with like-minded people to exchange tips and hints and to seek out solutions to problems. At work you could network with the same intent, only the common aim is for paid work purposes.

Everyone is good at something. What are you selling? What are you looking to 'buy'?

COMMUNICATION SKILLS

We network though communication, using verbal and non-verbal signals.

Verbal communication
These signals include:

- using questioning
- dealing with conflict
- problem-solving
- thinking skills
- awareness of feelings
- giving criticism.

Non-verbal communication
These signals include:

- voice tone
- voice volume
- voice pace
- facial expressions
- eye contact
- body stance

- listening skills
- gestures.

RELATIONSHIP SKILLS

Communication skills are only part of the story. How we actually relate to colleagues and those in authority will determine the co-operation we receive. Considerations within relationship skills include:

- gender expectations
- taking ownership for yourself
- increasing your chances of meeting people
- initiating conversation
- trust
- disclosing information about yourself
- defining yourself within a relationship.

GATHERING AND IMPARTING INFORMATION

A further skill in networking is the art of identifying the information you require, researching it and using it. The other side of this coin is making available to other people your reservoir of information and imparting it to them.

Networking is a mutual task. Naturally, we wouldn't be net-working if we didn't want something for ourselves. But we are more likely to find co-operation if we make networking a two-way operation.

CULTIVATING A NETWORK

Profitable networking happens over a period of time. As we go about our daily business at work, when socialising, on holiday, attending business conferences, we touch base and build contacts for the future.

When you're not working
If you aren't working at the moment, there are still ways of meeting

new people or building on existing contacts. The Jobcentre, Jobclubs, voluntary work, friends and family are a few ideas.

Building personal contacts

It's who you know that could prove useful. Family, friends, friends of friends, doctors, your local vet, friendly shopkeepers, down your local pub, places where you regularly eat out, support groups such as carers associations could all provide career networking opportunities.

Creating a support network

It is also important to build up a personal support network containing people you really trust who can provide a shoulder to cry on when times are tough. Use the following exercise to help you begin to identify a personal network:

Exercise: what is your personal support network?

• Who can provide me with a shoulder to cry on?

• Who can make me laugh when I feel down?

• Who can give me a hug when I need it?

• Who offers practical advice?

• Who can give me a philosophical slant when things go wrong?

• Who will listen to me without judging me?

Developing professional contacts

Building contacts with colleagues in your profession or trade is a life-line to potential work.

Think of people you admire in their working capacity. They may not necessarily be in the same line of work as yourself, but there is something about them that you admire.

If you are a woman in business, you may want to consider female role models with whom you could build a positive networking relationship. As a man in business, you need to consider the qualities you admire and cultivate networking relationships with the people who demonstrate those qualities.

CONCLUSION

You now have a brief overview of what career networking is about. The next step is relating networking to the new workplace. We live in a fast-changing business environment made complicated by technology, competition and the global marketplace. How do we, the workers, keep up to date with these changes? What impact will the new working trends have on us earning our living and what do we need to do to get ahead? These are some of the questions we will explore in the next chapter.

CASE STUDIES – AN INTRODUCTION

Carol wants to return to work
Carol is in her mid-thirties and wants to return to work after bringing up a family. She used to be a secretary but is totally out of touch with technology and modern office requirements. Training in word processing is one option, but she is open to exploring new ideas. Although a friendly person, Carol is shy when it comes to breaking new ground with strangers.

John's out of work
John is 29 and is a plumber and electrician by trade. He has been out of work for nine months. He is married with one young child. Because John can't get work, his wife is considering returning to work while he says at home looking after Ben. John is becoming increasingly moody and frustrated with his situation.

Iris wants to expand her business
Iris is in her late forties and is a freelance trainer in life-skills. She feels bored by her current contracts and wants to break out into something new.

DISCUSSION POINTS

1.   What were your initial images of networking before starting this book?

2.   Thinking back over your work history, how have you got work?

3.   What are the differences between the way the genders network? Do you network in a way typical of your gender?

2
Networking for the New Workplace

Most of us grew up with the 9–5, five days a week job which continued until retirement. Whenever we wanted a change there was always another job waiting. Now we have the opportunity to meet the challenge of change and to use the emergence of technology, skills development and the concept of having a composite career to our advantage.

UNDERSTANDING THE NEW COMPANY

Amin Rajan (*1990s: Where will the New Jobs Be?*, The Institute of Careers Guidance and the Centre for Research in Employment and Technology in Europe) has suggested that, as we head towards the twenty-first century, the following changes will take place:

- Firms will improve their competitiveness.

- The marketplace will increasingly cover a wider geographical and economic area.

- The workforce will have an emphasis on self-employed personnel.

- Alliances and networks between companies will increase.

- Organisations will involve themselves more through flexible structures involving teamwork and networking in the workplace.

- Women are likely to shift the gender composition of the workforce to their favour.

- The number of part-time jobs will increase.

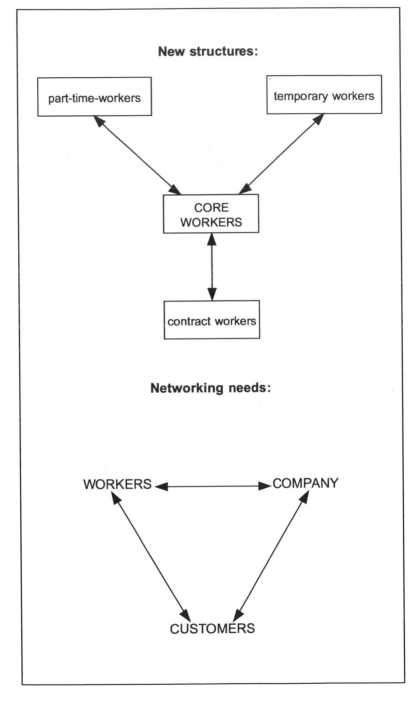

Fig. 3. The new company.

The smaller company

The large traditional company is disappearing and is being replaced by smaller sized companies with fewer traditional jobs. The new company offers various work projects bound together by workers using individual contractual arrangements such as teleworking, self-employment or part-time and temporary frameworks (see Figure 3).

The global marketplace

Firms will only be able to maintain or increase their levels of employment by improving their competitiveness. In favour of this, the marketplace will increasingly cover a wider geographical and economic area. Boundaries are breaking down the world over, creating a global marketplace. Employment structures are changing world-wide. If a business wants to survive, it needs to think in terms of other cultures, needs and market forces.

Increase in self-employment

As business practice becomes more streamlined, the workforce will have an emphasis on self-employed personnel. The permanent core of a company will be smaller, with non-essential work being contracted out to freelancers.

Networking

Alliances and networks between companies will increase, facilitating the creation of streamlined companies which rely on shared information. Organisations will not be so answerable to a hierarchical system of authority, but will involve itself more through flexible structures involving teamwork and networking in the workplace. The new company will rely on networking techniques to bind it together in order to:

- bring in new staff
- locate new customers
- interact with customers
- interact with other companies
- keep ahead of change.

Exercise: company networks
If you are working, how do the personnel in your company network with each other?

Changing role for women

Women are likely to shift the gender composition of the workforce to their favour. Because of the decrease in lower-skilled jobs and changes in the traditional working structure, women are better placed to be multi-skilled, supplying the workplace needs in a variety of flexible formats.

Increase in part-time workers

Although permanent, long-term work will be harder to get and the number of full-time jobs will decline, the number of part-time jobs is increasing all the time. A flexible workforce is required on almost all levels, giving rise to temporary, part-time, job-share and contract opportunities.

Your new role

You will need to be able to work without a clear job description and to prepare yourself for short-term employment. Staying in work means you will need to constantly demonstrate your value to the organisation in each situation you find yourself in. Your place within the new company is as the supplier, fulfilling a need to the customer (the employer).

WORKING IN NEW WAYS

The composite career

Because full-time, permanent work will become harder to get, the trend will be towards having two or three part-time jobs or contracts. Rather than the traditional 9–5 job, you are likely to have a composite career which has several strands running at the same time, starting and finishing ad hoc. In order to maintain your working life, you will need job-specific skills plus job-search skills.

Running your working life like a business

Learn to see every potential work situation as a market. Find new ways to exploit your skills, knowledge and experience and learn how to take advantage of opportunities to sell yourself.

The reality is that you are now in charge of your own career. You can learn new skills, no matter what your age (it is predicted that the workforce in employment is going to get older). The lower-skilled jobs are disappearing to be replaced by multi-skilled work opportunities. This suggests that the more versatile you are, the more likely you are to stay in work.

Flexible working

Growth rates will be greatest for women, part-time workers and the self-employed. Part-timers are likely to increase in distribution, transport, business and public services. You may think these flexible ways of working don't affect you or you may be already finding out that they do. Flexible working is set to grow and if you want to stay in work for as long as you choose, you will need to reorganise your working life to accommodate working in a different way.

Teleworking (working at home, for an employer, using computers, fax machine, modem and telephone), home working, outsourcing (being part of a temporary workforce for an employer) and interim (temporary) management are set to become a permanent fixture in a flexible working life.

Being a core worker

A core worker is someone who is probably aged between 25 and 45, they are likely to be career-minded, and working in the central part of an organisation, probably in management or project development. A core worker is full-time and will have an intense and heavy workload. Their career progression is likely to be seen as a series of high-powered jobs, not necessarily with the same organisation.

Being a contract worker

This type of worker is not a permanent, full-time member of staff. They will be self-employed and contracted in to do occasional specialist work. They are likely to work for more than one organisation.

Part-time and temporary work

- Nearly a quarter of UK employees are now employed on a part-time or temporary basis.

- Nine out of ten employers use part-time and temporary workers and over 70 per cent contract out non-core operations.

- A part-time or temporary worker is unlikely to be career-minded. They may be carers, have a family to bring up, be disabled or want variety without commitment.

Being self-employed

The number of people choosing to become self-employed has increased and is set to continue growing. You can never be made redundant from being self-employed. Your workload may decrease – but it can also increase. If the market for your business is shrinking, you can always change direction and start another business. Your earnings are as limitless as the effort you put into your business.

Networking for the small business is crucial. You would network with suppliers, customers, clients, manufacturers, journalists, publicity agents, accountants, bank personnel, solicitors, professional colleagues, graphic designers, the local council, chamber of commerce – the list is endless.

Exercise: How do you want to work?

Part-time   Do you want to job-share?

Temporary   Do you want casual work you can drop
               in and out of?

Core   Are you career-minded?
               Are you prepared to work long hours?

Contract   Are you a specialist?

PLANNING YOUR CAREER

Nowadays, each one of us has the opportunity to be in charge of our own working life. It is up to each person to plan their career and re-skill when appropriate.

Life-long learning

Because of the continuous movement between employment, you will need to plan a continuous learning programme for yourself which involves regular training. If you want to be in a position to be of service to employers, you need to know what they want and to be in a position to fulfil it. You need to know the skills and knowledge required and to have the skills and knowledge to sell.

Exercise: Learning goals

- What do you want to learn?

- Will your learning improve your work prospects? How?

- Do you want to learn by returning full or part-time to college?

- Do you want to go to university?

- Do you want to learn via distance/open learning?

- Can you afford to learn?

NETWORKING FOR WORK

Networking is vital to our working lives. It is only through interaction with others, through asking the right questions, listening, researching and being seen that we will be able to have a sense of control and security throughout a continuously changing working life.

Job leads

By building up our network of contacts, we can be in the know about vacancies and company requirements before they go on general release. Employers prefer to be recommended someone for a job because this means they don't have to have the cost of advertising and hassle of recruitment. Employers use their networks when they want workers as much as workers use each other to get in the back door. I have had at least two large contracts through being contacted by people who already knew of my training background. Both contracts helped me to develop management skills.

Goal setting relevant to career planning

Nowadays the average career lasts five years, so we need to be prepared to change direction on a fairly regular basis. In order to make informed decisions, we need to be aware of the choices. In order to be aware of the choices, we need to find out what they are – through networking. We might use career counsellors, the library, professional institutions, the local college or the local chamber of commerce. We might need to talk to people already experienced in the profession or trade we want to go into. Networking may attract a mentor, someone who has status and experience who can guide and advise us.

Decision-making

When we need to make decisions, we can sometimes feel overwhelmed by the sheer volume of considerations. Then we may need to network. Talking to friends or colleagues can help us get a slant on their experiences and viewpoints. We may need to network with a counsellor to clear the ground of emotional confusion before a decision can be reached.

Planning a continuous learning programme

In order to plan a learning programme for ourselves, we need to know what kind of courses are available, who pays for the training and the different ways in which we might to choose to train. We discover the facts by networking with colleges, universities, open learning institutions, the careers office or the Jobcentre. We need to make an ongoing commitment to training and therefore need to be aware of the current skills and knowledge in demand by our profession or trade.

Staying in control

Networking gives us a sense of control. In the ever-changing world of work, we can gain a sense of continuity by regularly contacting our network of people. Networking is not only about gathering and disseminating work-related information. It is also about feeling connected to like-minded people with whom we can exchange mutual support and encouragement.

Gaining visibility to potential employers

Networking means communicating, in person or by technology. When we communicate, we connect with another person and exchange thoughts, feelings, perceptions and ideas. We gain visibility. We define how we want to be seen. Others hear and see our professionalism, expertise, knowledge and enthusiasm and might want to buy.

Identifying new ways to exploit skills and knowledge

When we talk, we bounce ideas off each other. We stimulate and inspire each other to see another viewpoint. Networking provides an arena for experimenting.

Getting opportunities for work

While we are doing one job, there may be opportunities to do another. Networking gives us insight into what needs doing. One particular contract I had involved training special needs people for work. In addition, I recognised an opportunity to develop a learning programme which went alongside national standards, but modified it to the specific needs of the training group.

Diversifying skills and knowledge

By opening ourselves up to new experiences through networking, we have the opportunity to develop and diversify, thereby building up new skills.

Pursuing corporate goals

Whether we are a core worker or a contract worker, it is useful to network in order to gain an awareness of the corporate culture of the company we work for. When we understand the company vision, we are better able to contribute to fulfilling it.

Initiating action

When we have facts at our fingertips, we have more confidence and feel more in control. As our foundation becomes stronger, we can be pro-active and network to initiate action. We can approach that potential employer, we can enrol on that training course. We can take charge of our lives.

CONCLUSION

The scene is set. We understand the new workplace and how networking fits in. Now we need to ascertain what it is that we want from networking. What are we selling? Who is the buyer?

CASE STUDIES

Carol's lack of confidence

Carol's working background is quite traditional. Her mother works part-time in retail while her father buys and sells property. Carol's husband is a freelance computer consultant and trainer. A part-time job, maybe job-sharing, would suit Carol as she still needs to collect her young daughter from school. She lacks practical skills and career information at this point and feels a lack of confidence in pushing herself to find out more.

John's bored

When John works, he operates on a contractual basis. He isn't very self-motivated to find new contracts, believing that people will come to him and if they don't, this means the work isn't there to begin with. Basically, he's bored with his work but doesn't want to stay at home looking after his son either. As yet, he doesn't quite understand the value of being pro-active.

Iris wants a change

Iris is used to constantly looking out for new contracts, but she wants some kind of long-term commitment to project work. She understands the value of networking and that 'who you know will usually get you what you want'. At this point she is fulfilling her contractual arrangements, but not making any moves to change her situation.

DISCUSSION POINTS

1. What could be the benefits of having a composite career?

2. Consider the companies in your town which have expanded in the last two years. Would you consider working for them and why?

3. Take your last or current job and analyse the ways in which you kept yourself up to date with regard to skills, corporate decisions, *etc.*

3
Being Seen as a Specialist

At this stage, you should have some sense of what you want to buy out of the networking process – information, increase in skills, a job or promotion. In order to get the maximum rewards from networking, you need to be clear about what it is that you are selling – your skills, strengths and experience. This chapter is designed to help you focus on your 'toolbox' of skills and strengths. You need this toolbox to bargain with. In order to get what you want, you need to have the goods to sell. Your toolbox will also attract to you people who maybe don't have what you want at the moment, but want what you have. So you mark up a favour for the future.

FILLING THE SKILLS SHORTAGE

Most employers see an increasing need for skills. The most common reasons are changes in processes/technology and changes in work practices (Skills and Enterprise Executive, 1996). The skills most commonly thought to be lacking are practical skills, communication skills and personal skills.

Growth in demand in the higher-skilled occupations is predicted to the year 2000 and beyond and there is a growing emphasis on multi-skilling and quality (Department for Education and Employment).

The main reason for a skills shortage is the change in occupational trends towards higher-level occupations such as professional, managerial and technical posts. The work itself is requiring increased skills. The projected occupational changes favour white-collar, non-manual occupations. It is increasingly clear that the general skills content within most jobs is growing. The increase in skills demands within jobs is not restricted to specialist skills in specific jobs. The increasing emphasis on quality, innovation and customer care will demand more skills. In manufacturing there is an increasing requirement for people who can understand the wider production process (*Labour Market and Skills Trends 1996/1997*).

The *Skill Needs in Britain Survey 1995* shows that the skills needs

CLASSIFICATION	SKILLS SPECIFICS
Core skills	Literacy Numeracy Communication skills Self-motivation Organisational skills Self-management
Vocational skills	Skills/knowledge transferable between occupations, *eg*: IT skills supervisory/management customer care general vocational skills linguistic and cultural skills
Job-specific skills	Tasks and knowledge specific to a particular employer

Abstract skills	Self-awareness
	Self-promotion
	The ability to explore and create
	    opportunities
	Self-confidence
	The ability to transfer skills
	Strong development focus
	An ability to cope with uncertainty
	Political awareness
	Negotiation skills
	Decision-making skills
	Setting goals
	Action planning
	Networking
	Working in teams
	Working on several projects at once
	Planning a continuous learning
	    programme
	Being pro-active
	Diversification
	Flexibility
	Handling change
	Emotional resilience

Fig. 4. Developing the right skills.

of existing employees are rising. The report also suggests that the service sector in particular is more likely to observe the need for rising skills in its workforce.

Being multi-skilled

Job enlargement has brought about an increasing need for multiple skills. Job enlargement can be seen as taking on a larger number of roles at a similar level (*Labour Market and Skills Trends 1996/1997*).

Although companies are becoming more streamlined in order to compete in the global marketplace and redundancies are occurring, there is an increasing amount of work for the workers who are left. Core workers are expected to have a wide range of skills including leadership, managerial, developmental, professional and technical abilities. Freelancers who fill contractual roles can only stay in business if they have not only skills and knowledge in their particular line of expertise but also marketing and entrepreneurial abilities.

Transferring your skills

Transferable skills are identified abilities which you have developed through paid and unpaid work which can be moved between occupations, *eg* management and leadership skills. If you want to get maximum return from your networking, you need to be aware of giving your transferable skills a high profile.

IDENTIFYING SKILLS AND STRENGTHS

Skills can be broken down into four main areas: core, vocational, job-specific and abstract (see Figure 4).

Core skills

These are the skills which are formed by our general education and basic character. They include basic literacy and numeracy, relationship skills, our sense of purpose and how we motivate ourselves, how we organise our time and work and how we manage ourselves (psychologically and physically). Our awareness, knowledge and practice of these skills are contributed to by our early conditioning, our schooling and our peer group. They become more sophisticated as we mature into adulthood.

Vocational skills

These refer to the skills and knowledge transferable between occupations and are normally taught by employers or further and higher education.

Job-specific skills

These are built on top of vocational skills and refer to how an individual employer would want us to work for them using our vocational skills. They are more specific and focused and taught by employers.

Abstract skills

These refer to our attitude towards work, how we conduct ourselves within work and the personal qualities necessary to deal with the new workplace.

We need to be aware of what makes us tick in order to discover what motivates us in a work capacity. Do we develop our skills according to a basic need for money, in order to express part of ourselves or a mixture of both? We need to have confidence in our abilities, or if we lack skills, we need to have the confidence to go out and get them.

How good are you at research and exploring possibilities for training? Do you blindly stumble on getting skilled in what you fancy or do you research the market to see if there is a job with a future at the end of your study?

If we are to survive in the world of work, we need to be aware of commercial needs and the requirements of employers. We need to see ourselves as the supplier fulfilling an employer's needs. Having located potential work, we then need to market ourselves and negotiate terms.

Once in the job, you will be required to work on multi-levels, possibly handling a variety of tasks at once. You may be required to work on your own or in a team. You need to be versatile and have well-developed communication skills. Even when working, you need to have developmental strengths. You need to be continuously looking out for fresh opportunities – if not directly for yourself, then for your boss. If you can somehow bring in fresh business, this bodes well for you staying in work.

Through all this you need emotional resilience. Keeping in work is hard work. You need to be able to cope with uncertainty and constant change. These are the bolt-on skills, the abstract qualities needed for the new workplace. As well as vocational skills and job-specific skills, you will certainly need to stretch yourself to meet fresh challenges.

Skills for the IT society

If you wish to network as an IT specialist you need to be aware of marketing the following:

1. Invention skills   – necessary to invent and develop technology.

2. Exploitative skills – needed to see where and how technology can be used.

3. Adaptation skills – to make sure that the technology can be used in the workplace.

4. Usage skills   – getting the desired benefits.

(Taken from *The Developing Skills of the Information Society*, TeamConsulting.)

Anyone wanting to increase their job prospects needs to be aware of the information age. Skills are necessary in the areas of how information is accessed and communicated, not only for personal career networking purposes but also for the efficient running of any business. As the core of businesses becomes more streamlined and the workforce becomes more scattered via freelancers, part-time and temporary outlets, communicating information takes on a key role.

EVALUATING YOUR SKILLS

Below are six project boxes to help you build up your skills toolbox:

- IT skills

- Leadership skills

- Customer care skills

- General vocational skills

- Linguistic and cultural skills

- Abstract skills.

PROJECT 1. IT skills

What software packages can I use?

Can I use the internet?

Am I experienced in computer network systems?

Have I programming experience?

Have I experience of teleworking?

PROJECT 2. Leadership skills and strengths
Which of the following skills and strengths do I have?

listening

focus

decisiveness

motivating others

developing vision

setting long-term goals

acknowledging accomplishments
   of others

giving genuine feedback to
   others

promoting team effort

strategic planning

planning work

marketing

managing my resources

report writing

skills training

employee relations

building and developing the team

counselling

project management

IT management

use of languages

team building

stockholder focus

technical change

directness

accessibility

taking risks

solving problems

being pro-active

delegating tasks

acknowledging my mistakes

sharing my power

looking for challenges

setting objectives

financial management

allocating work

quality management

interviewing/induction of
   new employees

performance appraisal

making decisions

coaching

global marketplace
   awareness

staff development

customer orientation

assessing

managing change

business unit focus

PROJECT 3. Customer care skills

Do I have the following skills?

listening   problem solving
working as part of the team   questioning

PROJECT 4. General vocational skills

Which of the following have I been trained in or do I have extensive experience of?

Communications, *eg* journalism, publishing.

Construction, *eg* building, electrical, heating and ventilation.

Developing skill and knowledge, *eg* teaching, training.

Engineering, *eg* aeronautical, electric power, telecommunications, vehicle maintenance.

Natural resources, *eg* gas, petroleum oil and gas technology, water treatment and supply.

Manufacturing.

Providing business services, *eg* banking, computer services, insurance, administration.

Providing services and goods, *eg* beauty, food and drink, tourism, sport and recreation.

Providing health and social care, *eg* child care, housing, probation work.

Providing protective services, *eg* armed forces, security.

Tending land, animals and plants, *eg* agriculture, animal care, landscape design.

Transport, *eg* distribution.

PROJECT 5. Linguistic and cultural skills

Which languages can I speak with confidence?

Which cultures do I feel comfortable working within?

PROJECT 6. Abstract skills

How good am I at selling my skills to potential employers?

Do I bounce back quickly after a disappointment?

Can I do several tasks at once?

Do I enjoy working in teams?

Am I a self-starter?

Can I set realistic goals?

Am I aware of how political trends affect the economy?

EVALUATING YOUR ACHIEVEMENTS

An additional bonus to your toolbox are your achievements. Potential employers like to know what you have done in the past as it indicates what you could do for them in the future. Do you have a track record of:

- cutting costs
- developing staff performance
- increasing sales
- cutting staff costs
- meeting deadlines easily
- providing more information
- improving teamwork
- improving the appearance of something
- turning round a negative situation
- avoiding potential problems
- opening up more potential
- making the boss look good?

USING YOUR STRENGTHS

Your strengths describe your personal qualities. As well as what you can do, part of your sales pitch is what you are like as a person. Look at the qualities listed in the box below and tick those you think apply to you.

PERSONAL QUALITIES

adaptable	aggressive	ambitious	assertive	calm
caring	cautious	competitive	concise	confident
conscientious	creative	decisive	dedicated	dependable
determined	diplomatic	dynamic	easy going	efficient
encouraging	energetic	enterprising	extrovert	fair
firm	flexible	friendly	hardworking	helpful
initiator	innovative	intuitive	lateral thinker	leader
logical	methodical	meticulous	objective	ordered
organised	outgoing	patient	perceptive	persuasive
practical	precise	pro-active	resourceful	

MANAGING YOUR PROFESSIONAL IMAGE

As you build your toolbox of skills and strengths to barter with on the network circuit, you need to cultivate a positive and confident image with which to present your toolbox.

Skills

You need to be constantly aware of and updating your vocational skills so that you are in touch with current developments in your profession or trade. By being current or even ahead of developments you are gaining the advantage over your competitors.

Personal strengths

By cultivating self-awareness you are demonstrating a sense of confidence about who you are and this is communicated on the open market, suggesting you know what you are talking about. This in turn makes others want to know you, they want to have you on their side, they want your skills and knowledge working for them.

Building a reputation

Successful career networking means building a good reputation for yourself. A good reputation means you are someone worth knowing. A good reputation is built up and earnt through desirable skills and personal qualities.

Being seen as a specialist is one strand of your career networking strategy. But no matter how brilliant your skills, how extensive your experience or how many letters you have after your name, if you can't communicate with another person, no one is going to know about you.

CREATING YOUR PERSONAL PROFILE

How would you describe your skills, strengths and experience in a short paragraph (verbal or written)? Look at the following examples before writing your own.

Some examples of personal profiles

1. 'A Class 1 HGV driver with experience of delivering all types of food and non-perishable goods throughout the UK. A self-motivated individual with organisational skills and problem-solving ability.'

2. 'I am a good communicator and have a mature, caring attitude. I am able to get on well with people and have good listening skills. I am considered a quick learner able to acquire new skills and ideas easily. I am highly motivated and well organised with a conscientious approach.'

3. 'I have experience of both a commercial environment and the retail industry. I particularly enjoy the retail trade as I like customer contact which enables me to use my communication and inter-personal skills. I am used to managing staff and consequently a proficient organiser. I have a wide knowledge of commercial practices on the continent and am looking to develop my skills further.'

4. 'I am proficient in all aspects of office work and have excellent keyboard skills. I have experience of WordPerfect, Word for Windows and Excel. I work well within a team or on my own initiative and can organise my time effectively. I am highly motivated, take pride in my work and enjoy challenges.'

CONCLUSION

You have pinpointed what it is that you are selling. Your 'toolbox' is your bartering substance. This is what you wish to use in exchange for power, money or kudos. You want to be seen as an expert in order to get what you want. Equally you have these skills to help others in their bartering. Now you need to tell other people about yourself, your skills and what you want. You need also to be able to listen and respond to the needs of others. This is where you reach out and make contact.

CASE STUDIES

Carol has some unexpected skills

Carol has had secretarial experience and is familiar with basic office procedure and keyboarding, but she is out of touch with current information technology. As her husband is a computer consultant and trainer, she has picked up some awareness of word processing and other software applications. Her core skills are well developed and she has picked up useful bolt-on skills through being a mother and running a household, such as budgeting and time management. She has also been learning French at adult education classes just for the fun of it. Carol has also been a volunteer at her local toy library and so has begun to build her customer care skills.

John feels resentful

John is good at working with his hands. He doesn't feel too comfortable with words and numbers. Once he gets into a job, he knows his stuff but his communication skills are limited – he prefers working with things rather than people. Because he has rather lost interest in his trade he hasn't bothered to keep up to date with new technology. He therefore feels left behind and out of things. He is the sort of person who wants to be given the work so that he can get on with it. He feels resentful about having to develop abstract skills just to get work.

Iris is a leader

Iris has developed good vocational and abstract skills as a life-skills trainer. Her leadership skills are used to facilitate groups of adult students, her customer care skills have been used to get new contracts and she is a qualified trainer.

DISCUSSION POINTS

1. What is a knowledge-based working society?

2. Which of your current skills could be transferred to other occupations?

3. How might you describe yourself, in terms of what you do, to a total stranger?

4
Improving Your People Skills

Career networking is built upon communication. Communication covers a wide variety of methods we use to impart and receive information. An exercise I often give delegates attending a career development workshop is to 'think of at least fifteen ways to communicate'. The initial reaction is limited, but at the end of a brainstorming session the list looks something like the following:

WAYS TO COMMUNICATE

smoke signals	fax	Internet	eye contact
hand gestures	telephone	telepathy	flipchart
reading	writing	scribbling	screaming
whistling	fighting	e-mail	letter
music	art	sex	morse-code
semaphore	Braille	crying	touch
video	TV	cinema	mediumship
smell	body language	language	sign language
telex	advertisement	newspaper	

DEFINING PEOPLE SKILLS
Networking is about people skills. People skills are the methods we use to communicate with each other. Speaking to someone is a personal and instant interaction where thoughts and feelings can be directly expressed. Interpersonal skills are another way to describe the process.

People skills involve a set of behavioural styles. Figure 5 sets out four categories of behaviours. You might recognise some of them from Chapter 3 as personal qualities. Find out which one you show most of. Then read on to find out how to interact with different styles.

Behavioural Styles

Groupie	Doer	Thinker	Creator
accessible	aggressive	cautious	ambitious
adaptable	assertive	concise	creative
caring	competitive	conscientious	curious
calm	confident	dedicated	dramatic
courteous	decisive	dependable	excitable
diplomatic	determined	efficient	extrovert
discreet	dynamic	enquiring	flexible
easy going	energetic	fussy	humorous
empathic	enterprising	impartial	imaginative
encouraging	firm	logical	innovative
fair	initiator	methodical	intuitive
friendly	leader	meticulous	inventive
helpful	hardworking	objective	lateral thinker
likeable	practical	ordered	visionary
outgoing	pro-active	organised	
perceptive	resourceful	patient	
persuasive	strong-willed	precise	

Fig. 5. Which behavioural style are you?

46

Groupies

A Groupie is someone who needs to relate in order to get a sense of self. They enjoy interaction and find other people reassuring. When relating to a Groupie:

● find some area of common ground

● be responsive to their contributions.

Doers

Doers need to get results. They seldom involve themselves in idle chit-chat and want to get on with the job. When interacting with a Doer:

● deal in facts

● be specific.

Thinkers

A Thinker will deal in facts and logic. They are likely to be cautious and lean towards perfectionism. When communicating with a Thinker:

● be accurate

● produce practical evidence.

Creators

Creators are instinctive and creative with a low threshold of boredom. When relating to a Creator:

● be stimulating and fun

● provide extra angles to work with.

USING YOUR SENSORY SYSTEMS

We can further understand about communication and people skills by using our sensory system.

● Do you communicate primarily through mental images?
  – Do you use phrases like 'I get the picture' or 'Look at it like this'?
  – Do you pick up information through what you see and read?

- Do you communicate mainly through sound?
  - Do you use phrases like 'That sounds right to me' or 'I'd like to voice an opinion'?
  - Do you tend to retain information that you hear?

- Do you communicate through feelings and touch?
  - Do you say 'That feels right to me' or 'Let's keep in touch'?
  - Do you learn best when allowed to try things out for yourself?

COMMUNICATING WITH YOURSELF

'It was hard to communicate with you. You were always busy communicating with yourself. The line was busy.'

(Jean Kurr)

When we continually look inside of ourselves in an obsessed manner, no one else can get in and we can't get out. There is a breakdown in communication.

Successful career networking is about firstly communicating with yourself so that you understand what makes you tick, and then communicating with other people.

WORKING WITH GENDER DIFFERENCES

Networking is about all sorts of people relating to all sorts of other people. We all relate differently. For example, there are communication characteristics sometimes associated more with one gender than the other (see Figure 6).

Men tend to argue, interrupt, give instruction, respond to problems with solutions. Phrases they might use include:

- 'go for the throat'

- 'flag it up'

- 'reaching a target'.

Women tend to respond to problems with empathy, they use a helping format or bridge differences, they tend to negotiate and co-operate more than men. Phrases women might use include:

- 'I want to share this with you.'

- 'I get a sense of confusion.'

- 'What can we do about this problem?'

Female communication characteristics	Male communication characteristics
negotiates	decisive
asks questions with emotional	aggressive
overtones	analytical
mediates	assertive
quietly spoken	competitive
listens	defensive
affectionate	forceful
compassionate	dominant
uses gentle language	gives instructions
understands	solution orientated
sympathetic	interrupts
co-operative	

Fig. 6. Genderspeak.

USING COMMUNICATION

There are a number of reasons why we might want to communicate.

To be a catalyst

We may want to provoke self-discovery in others. If someone comes to us as part of their networking process, we may need to draw out of them what it is they really need from us.

To inform

We might need to impart information to someone who requires our expertise or we may need to tell someone what it is we require from them.

To support

Career networking is also about affirming each others' worth.

To act as a directive

We could be in a position to guide the behaviour of others, maybe to act as a coach or mentor in a networking system.

To release

We may need to help another to work through difficult issues along a career pathway.

USING AND READING BODY LANGUAGE

Using body language is an unspoken but vital part of communication. People skills are all about reading both the verbal and the non-verbal (see Figure 7). Body language can say what words can't. It can show you where there are contradictions in words. It can provide encouragement.

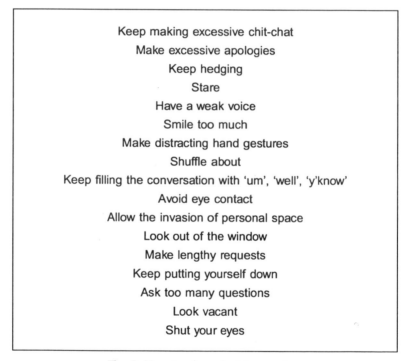

Keep making excessive chit-chat

Make excessive apologies

Keep hedging

Stare

Have a weak voice

Smile too much

Make distracting hand gestures

Shuffle about

Keep filling the conversation with 'um', 'well', 'y'know'

Avoid eye contact

Allow the invasion of personal space

Look out of the window

Make lengthy requests

Keep putting yourself down

Ask too many questions

Look vacant

Shut your eyes

Fig. 7. How to give a bad impression.

Factfile

Practising T'ai Chi, Alexander Technique, yoga and other forms of postural exercise and meditation can give you an upright, relaxed and balanced posture which in turn will give you internal confidence.

Going by appearance

You make an impression during the first three minutes of entering a room. Dress, appearance and grooming combine to give other people an instant, visual image of who you are.

What image do you want to give?				
casual	hippy	power dresser	trendy	student
sex kitten	business-like	macho	feminine	mysterious
sugar daddy	glamorous	designer-label	weirdo	artist
harassed executive	mad professor	college lecturer	mother earth	ethnic

Using touch

A person's handshake can tell you about their attitude. Do you recognise the limp handshake, the soggy palm routine, the handcrusher? What initial impression do you form about people with certain handshakes?

The right proximity

The more formal the relationship, the further away we tend to stand from each other. As a relationship develops, so the space between decreases. Physical barriers such as desks or podiums also represent proximity (or lack of it).

Watching the face

Anger can make someone go red or white. Red tends to indicate a more apparent anger whereas someone who has gone white with anger is more unpredictable. Eye contact is vital in imparting a sense of confidence and trustworthiness. Glaring may indicate anger while evasive eye action could indicate dishonesty or shyness. The more intimately we know a person, the further down their body our gaze goes. With business acquaintances we tend to look in a t-shape, across the eyes and down to the mouth. With intimate partners, who knows how far down we might look! Be aware of smiling to appease anger in someone else or having a fixed smile born out of sheer nerves.

Hand gestures

Someone waving their hands around can be trying to distract you from what they are saying. If you are a woman in male company and the man runs his hand down his tie this could mean he is attracted to you! Touching the nose or mouth while speaking may indicate that you're not telling the truth, while touching the ear could show that you're not sure about what you are hearing.

Body stance
Crossed arms and legs indicate a closed mind while an open body shows an open mind. When you are sitting down with someone and their legs are crossed towards you they're interested in what you have to say. If you are standing with your feet directed towards the person you are with, you are showing friendliness.

READING THE VOICE

If a person is tense, their voice might be high or fast. Anger might reflect in a harsh voice that wants to over-ride everyone else's. Someone who is shy or doubtful might come across monotonic (a droning sound all in one tone), mumbled or stuttering.

The emphasis you give words can alter the meaning of a sentence:

- *Are* you singing tonight? – This implies a level of disbelief.

- Are *you* singing tonight? – This suggests the questioner wants to know if that person in particular is singing.

- Are you *singing* tonight? – This implies a questioning of an action.

- Are you singing *tonight*? – This suggests impatience.

You need to be aware also of the level at which you are pitching your language.

MIRRORING ANOTHER PERSON

Mirroring is the art of matching some of your behaviours to that of the other person in order to get into their world. It is possible to match body stance, facial expressions, voice tone, pitch and volume, gestures, eye contact, verbal behaviour and even the breathing.

Exercise: Give examples of how people show the following feelings, using verbal and non-verbal behaviour.

- Willing to listen and be friendly.

- Anxious to interrupt.

- Feeling frustrated.

- Feeling rejected.

- Feeling threatened.

- Feeling superior.

- Not wishing to communicate.

USING QUESTIONS

> I kept six honest serving men,
> They taught me all I knew,
> Their names are WHAT and WHY and WHEN,
> And HOW and WHERE and WHO.
>
> (Rudyard Kipling)

How we ask questions will determine the answers we are given. Career networking is about giving and receiving answers which will help us achieve our working objectives. Therefore we need to ask questions which open up opportunities for helpful answers. For example:

- Elaboration questions give the other person a chance to expand

1 = poor	2 = occasionally good	3 = good

Communication skill	Own assessment	Assessment from colleague
Using questions		
Using touch		
The right proximity		
Dealing with conflict		
Problem-solving		
Thinking skills		
Awareness of feelings		
Giving criticism		
Mirroring		
Using hand gestures		
Listening skills		
Body stance		
Eye contact		
Facial expressions		
Voice pace		
Voice tone		
Voice volume		

Fig. 8. How strong are your communication skills?

on their subject.

● Specification questions draw out thoughts and feelings on a problem area.

● Personal responsibility questions allow the other person to contribute a sense of responsibility about resolving a problem.

DEVELOPING GOOD LISTENING SKILLS

Hearing is a natural activity (pending any health problems), but listening is not. We don't always listen to what is being said by another person. We can be tied up with our own thoughts and feelings which may or may not be relevant to what the speaker is talking about. If the other person presses our buttons and causes a powerful internal reaction, this can block our listening skills. Being with unsafe people can hinder our listening. We may be so tied up with coping with feelings of anxiety we shut our listening faculties down. Having something we are dying to say can impede listening. Sometimes people may listen to avoid talking and revealing themselves.

What might interfere with someone listening?
sight difficulties   hearing problems
distraction of noise   memory difficulties
low intelligence   daydreaming
tiredness   ill health
prejudice   anxiety
fear   short attention span
boredom   dislike
anger   not understanding

ASSESSING YOUR COMMUNICATION SKILLS

Using the table in Figure 8, assess your own communication skills. then ask a work colleague to give their own rating of you.

CONCLUSION

There is nothing so constant as change. You are constantly using and developing your people skills. Each day you interact and communicate with others. And you can deepen your understanding and experience of communication and use your skills to become a more assertive and powerful person in your networking.

CASE STUDIES

Carol is emotional

Carol likes to be with people and sees herself as a Groupie. She communicates largely through feelings and sound and sees herself relating in typically female ways.

John is a man's man

John is a Thinker and tends to see the world in mental images. He feels uncomfortable with feelings and is more relaxed when communicating with men.

Iris is a doer

Iris communicates mainly through mental images and sees herself as a Doer. She feels happier communicating with men.

DISCUSSION POINTS

1. What did you learn about people skills from your parents?

2. Define the different ways in which you communicate with the various people in your life?

3. How has the way in which your gender communicates changed over the past ten years?

5
Becoming More Assertive

DEFINING ASSERTIVENESS

Career networking is based on good communication. But network-ing opportunities can be further developed through assertive behaviour (see Figure 9).

Why are we unassertive?

There are many influences which affect how we come to think of ourselves. Some include the family, especially parents and siblings. Additional influences include teachers and community leaders. Our peer group influences our sense of self. If we were constantly criticised by influential people when we were young, this can undermine our self-esteem. If our individuality was not encouraged and valued, this would make us feel worthless and unimportant. Other considerations include our position in the family. If you are the oldest, you may feel a strong sense of responsibility for others even as an adult. As the youngest, you may feel unimportant in the pecking order. The kind of schooling you had might influence your sense of confidence, as might what you achieved at school. Our gender and social class are further influences on our sense of self-esteem. As a child did you have a role model of assertive behaviour or were the role models aggressive or passive?

Recognising the victim

A victim is someone who believes that everything that happens to them is the fault of someone else. They have abdicated personal responsibility and behave as if they have no control over what happens to them. A victim feels small, helpless and powerless and will allow other people to control their personal space. A victim will wait for networking contacts to come to them or they might think they have nothing to contribute to a networking system. They might believe the world owes them a living or they might believe they don't deserve one in the first place.

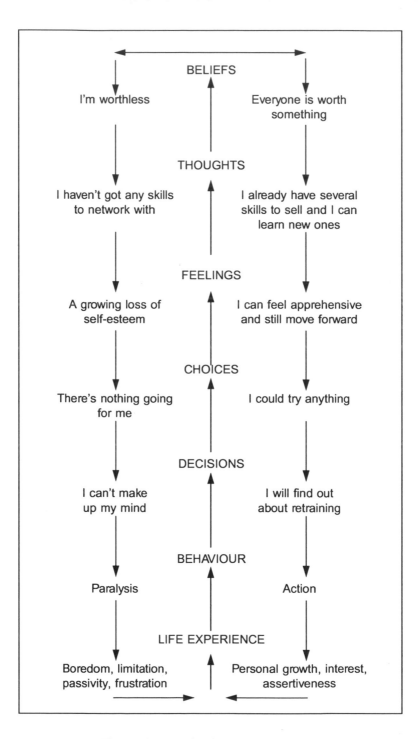

BELIEFS

I'm worthless   Everyone is worth something

THOUGHTS

I haven't got any skills to network with   I already have several skills to sell and I can learn new ones

FEELINGS

A growing loss of self-esteem   I can feel apprehensive and still move forward

CHOICES

There's nothing going for me   I could try anything

DECISIONS

I can't make up my mind   I will find out about retraining

BEHAVIOUR

Paralysis   Action

LIFE EXPERIENCE

Boredom, limitation, passivity, frustration   Personal growth, interest, assertiveness

Fig. 9. The assertive (or unassertive) loop.

Recognising the aggressor

An aggressor is someone who is dominant and needs to be in control. They come over as loud and large. Someone who is aggressive is often hiding someone who is frightened of feeling small and vulnerable. An aggressor will invade another person's personal space in an effort to control them before they are controlled. An aggressor would feel as if other people are there for the aggressor's purpose. The aggressor will take but not give.

Assertive networking

Assertiveness is directly telling someone what you want and negotiating with them for a mutually satisfying outcome. It is about being open and standing up for your rights while realising that other people share those same rights. An assertive person has a strong sense of personal power and confidence.

An assertive person is someone who is aware of their own thoughts, feelings and behaviours. They take responsibility for themselves. An assertive person recognises they have control only over themselves and not over any other person. Because an assertive person is in charge of themselves, they are confident. Being confident doesn't mean never feeling negative or down. It means having the confidence to recognise and accept that not feeling OK sometimes is a natural part of being human. We live a life of peaks and troughs and being assertive and confident means accepting the highs and lows as part of our experiences.

Question time

● When was the last time you gave away your personal power in a working situation?

● How did you feel when you last used your power in a working situation?

OVERCOMING SELF-DOUBT

Self-doubt can be like a little demon whispering in your ear, telling you how awful you are. Taking responsibility means making conscious that inner voice of self-doubt and changing its negative messages to positive ones. Think for a moment of all the things you might say to yourself:

'I'm not good enough.'
'I can't do that.'
'No one will ever listen to me.'
'I never stand up for myself.'

Does that critical inner voice:

- Suggest that others don't like you and are determined to sabotage your entire life?

- Use exaggerated negative descriptions?

- Insist on paying attention to only small parts of your experience?

- Insist that everything you do must be fantastic otherwise you're a failure?

- Suggest you're responsible for things outside your control?

These critical messages distort our sense of self-esteem and can hold us back from accepting our skills and strengths and making contact with others for networking purposes. In order to increase confidence, we need to reduce the power of this inner critic by understanding why some of its messages are potentially damaging and find positive ways of contradicting its negative messages. Using affirmations can be one effective way. Using short phrases to counteract each negative message from the inner critic can help to reassure us. For example:

'I'm not good enough.'   'I HAVE GOOD TRAINING
                                SKILLS.'

'No one will want to   'SOMEONE MIGHT WANT
hear from me.'   MY SKILLS RIGHT NOW.'

Building self-esteem
Take the time to list your strengths under the following headings:

- *Three successes* (*eg* bringing in a new client).

- *Three difficulties I handled well* (*eg* turning round a difficult customer and selling her a more expensive TV).

- *Three times I have been thanked or congratulated* (*eg* finishing a particular project ahead of schedule).

- *Three responsibilities I shoulder well* (*eg* the monthly cash flow).

Project
- List the negative messages you give yourself about work.

- Create some positive messages which could raise your self-esteem.

DEFINING OWNERSHIP

Taking responsibility for our thoughts, feelings and behaviour means we are adults. It isn't always easy to be an adult. Often we react emotionally and irrationally, causing ourselves and others distress. Ownership means owning ourselves. Not blaming another. Not being flopsie-bunnie and rolling over.

Using the 'I' word
When we converse with someone, we often use another person to express our own thoughts or feelings, *eg* 'they always say it's better to give than receive' or 'he made me really angry'. In reality we are saying 'I think it is better to give than to receive' and 'I feel really angry'. There are two ways to use the word. The first is in a self-centred way 'I want, I feel, I will'. The unspoken words are 'I don't give a monkeys what the rest of you think, feel or want'. The second is the assertive and confident way of using it: 'I feel uncomfortable about this situation, how do you feel?' The second way is owning the feelings and also respecting the rights of others to have feelings.

Use 'I' when disclosing feelings, thoughts and actions. You are showing responsibility for owning them and also acknowledging your separateness to another. This approach will engender less defensiveness in someone else.

MAKING CONTACT

Getting started on your networking programme involves making opportunities as well as taking opportunities.

Project: making contacts
List as many ways as possible that you might increase your chances of meeting useful people.

Barriers to making contact

Your skills may be ready and waiting to be bartered, your communication is honed to perfection, but still you may feel unwilling to push yourself forward. There are mental barriers in the way of physical action. Exploring your beliefs about initiating relationships may help to refocus your thinking. Consider the following:

1. I am not prepared to take risks.
2. Women shouldn't initiate relationships.
3. I get anxious about meeting people I don't know well.
4. I tend to wait for other people to initiate a relationship.
5. I can't be myself with new people.
6. I judge people too quickly on first impressions.
7. I am frightened of being rejected.
8. I must not ask for what I want.
9. Others might take advantage of me
10. Others might think I'm pushy.

All of the above could act as barriers to starting new relationships.

Making a request

As you become clearer about your networking requirements, you can begin to reach out and make contact. You need to:

- clarify your objective

- identify a contact person and their telephone number, address, fax or e-mail address

- recognise opportunities at meetings or conferences

- approach your networking contact stating who you are, any mutual colleagues, what you require and how you can be contacted.

Some people may try to fob you off but you can come back with an assertive response:

Other person	*Your response*
'I can't help, I've got too much to do.'	'I understand that you are busy at the moment. When would it be convenient to come and see you?'

Networking action cards project
Begin a Network Index Box, writing contact names and details
on cards, as in the example in Figure 10.

NAME	Jonathan Whistler
PHONE NUMBER	01234 567890
FAX NUMBER	01234 987654
E-MAIL ADDRESS	cfde@cfde.plonk.co.uk
ADDRESS	37 Anywhere Street, Somewhere Town, Sussex
INFORMATION THEY HAVE	Editorial contacts in the publishing industry

Fig. 10. Example networking action card.

Being persistent

If you feel someone isn't listening to you, but you are very clear
about what you need to say, try using the **broken record technique**:

- Identify your goal.

- Get the other person's attention by saying a 'I'd like you to listen
  to me.'

- Make a clear statement: 'I would like the name of the person who
  can help me.'

- Repeat the statement if necessary.

Relating to authority

Career networking will mean, at some point, relating to authority.
A fear of authority figures may cause us to fear criticism or feel
inadequate. We may see them as having unrealistic expectations of
us and fear we cannot meet their expectations. However, authority
figures at work could be in a very useful and powerful position to
help us achieve our networking goals. As we feel more comfortable
with authority figures, we begin to act with increased self-esteem,
accept constructive criticism and behave more assertively. We
understand that those in authority have their own fears and
insecurities. We start to evaluate situations and choose our
behaviour and responses rather than just reacting.

	Aggressive	Passive	Assertive
Voice	firm, sarcastic, loud, hard, sharp, strident	wobbly, whining, monotonic, quiet	steady, firm, clear, controlled
Speech	abrupt, fast, clipped	hesitant, jerky, throat swallowing	fluent, steady, emphasising key words
Face	scowling, chin forward	ghost smile, quick changing features	open, non-verbal and verbal agreement
Eyes	staring, slit	looking down, evasive	firm, direct
Gestures	finger pointing or stabbing or thumping	hand wringing, covering mouth, fiddling	open hands
Body	striding round, invasive of body space	hunched shoulders, steps back, arms crossed, feet shuffling	sits/stands upright, head up
Verbal	excessive use of 'I', boasting, threatening, put downs, sarcasm, blame, ignoring response, interrupting	rambling, self put downs, apologetic, justification, allowing interruptions	brief, clear, direct, problem-solving questions, constructive criticism, negotiating

Fig. 11. How do you come across?

Criticism from others

Criticism from others can sometimes be hard to take, especially if it is delivered without thought or feeling. This might lead to us feeling a lack of confidence or undervalued with regard to our strengths and skills. However, career networking does open us to opportunities which may involve other people commenting upon our skills.

Negative assertion
It is possible to gain personal understanding about ourselves if we use a technique called **negative assertion**. This is where we assertively accept something which is negative about ourselves by understanding that a mistake is only a mistake. A criticism does not imply we are a worthless human being. It suggests that a particular behaviour or attitude is not helpful to us. But it is our responsibility to determine whether or not the criticism is valid, either in part or in whole. The idea is to accept the problem and focus on what is to be done about it.

'You need to get out and network for more contacts.'

'I network a little already, but I could certainly get myself out and about a bit more.'

Negative inquiry
You could use the technique of **negative inquiry** to prompt further criticism about yourself by asking for more information, about yourself or your behaviour. Someone may say to you: 'I'm not sure your management style would suit the new team'. Your reply could be: 'How do you see my management style at the moment?'

Further tips on dealing with criticism
- Count to ten.
- Develop problem-solving skills.
- Assess whether the criticism is really worth following up.
- Ask for time and come back to the person.
- Clear up any misunderstandings.

Project
During the next week, ask two people to criticise your working practices.

I have the right:

● to ask for information

● to expect honesty from others

● to be treated with dignity and respect

● to express my own standards and values

● to say I don't understand

● to be successful

● to change and grow

● to determine my own priorities.

Fig. 12. The assertive networking charter.

DEVELOPING A NETWORKING ETHOS

Showing appreciation

Some people find it difficult to accept compliments upon their behaviour or skills. If we shrug off a genuine compliment we are throwing a verbal gift back in someone's face. Just agree by saying 'Thank you, I get a lot of satisfaction from dealing with customer queries.'

You might use a technique called **positive inquiry** to find out more information about something someone likes or thinks you have done well.

Using feedback

Networking relationships are developed through the constructive giving and receiving of feedback. When you give feedback, communicate the positive, describe the value of what has happened and express your appreciation for the person's behaviour:

'Thank you for considering me when you were recruiting for the new administrator. I welcomed the opportunity of coming along for an interview. I hope we will work together in the future.'

Being positive

- Isolate destructive words such as 'only' and 'just'.

- Take mental control and turn the negative messages into positive ones.

- Accentuate the positive.

- Change to an active and problem-solving framework.

- Recognise opportunities.

- Identify positive role models.

- Develop your interests and skills.

- Learn to like who you are.

CONCLUSION

Networking is the gaining of knowledge and information. The next stage is how we can identify the right information and how we can gather the information together in order to make the best use of it.

> **Never keep a networking contact longer than the potential to teach each other something.**

CASE STUDIES

Carol's on the defensive

Carol is assertive with her family but passive outside it. When she is sure of her ground she is confident. Her initial response to low confidence is to be aggressive and attack.

John's uncomfortable with women

When John is amongst men he is confident. When he is with women, he becomes either passive or aggressive.

Iris likes to be in control

Iris can appear to be a little aggressive at times. This is a natural part of her personality. When she is in a group as a peer sometimes she can seem passive.

DISCUSSION POINTS

1. Describe the different types of assertive, passive and aggressive behaviour as demonstrated by men and women. Are you typical of your gender?

2. When can self-doubt be useful?

3. What is the link between our experiences of our parents and any current fears we have of authority figures?

6
Gathering Information

Career networking is about identifying. gathering and utilising information. It is also about imparting information.

ESTABLISHING OBJECTIVES

You should by now have begun establishing why you want to gather information.

Being out of work

Have you been made redundant? Are you out of work? Do you want to increase your contacts in order to get back to work? Information you might find useful could include:

- employers moving into your locality

- people leaving their job and creating a vacancy

- how to get retrained (perhaps free of cost)

- how to write speculative letters

- how to write a CV

- how to improve your interview techniques

- how to claim all your entitled benefits

- how to become self-employed

- where to get funding.

Wanting promotion

Maybe you are looking to move up into management or you would like to apply for a more challenging and interesting job within your company. You might look out for:

- information on in-house training courses

- internal vacancies

- someone who could act as a mentor.

Coming back after a career break

Maybe you are returning to the workplace after a career break or bringing up a family. Information on the following might prove useful:

- returning to study

- how to work for yourself

- flexible ways of working

- childcare

- interview techniques

- CV writing

- jobsearch skills.

Needing to learn new skills

You may be in the position of job enlargement (where people have left but not been replaced and the people who are left are doing more work). This is a time of opportunity where you can increase your skills base. In order to take advantage of this, you might want:

- information on in-house training

- a mentor to guide you

- a coach to instruct you

- information on college courses.

Wanting to become self-employed

You may be newly redundant or you may be fed up working for other people. Self-employment is a two-pronged attack – your good idea and the business skills to run and develop it. There is no point in having the best idea since sliced bread if all flounders on a lack of business acumen. Information that might prove useful could include:

- raising capital

- how to do your own marketing

- building a team of professionals for back-up, *eg* accountant
- premises and equipment
- tax, insurance and other financial matters.

IDENTIFYING SOURCES OF INFORMATION

Now you know **why** you want information and you know **what** kind of information. So **where** do you go to find it and **who** can help you?

The media
The media can provide a good source of information. Consider also trade journals and magazines published by professional associations.

Newspapers
Your local newspaper is packed with information. The situations vacant section not only offers jobs but also the opportunity to network. For instance, I saw a display ad in our local press for a full-time features writer for a business magazine. I didn't want a full-time position, so I offered myself as a freelance writer. I've now written five articles for them. You could use the situations vacant section to provide contacts for a speculative letter.

News items also provide information about companies moving in and out of your area. Look at the advertisements for goods or services. Make contact – they might tell you something lucrative!

Periodicals
Magazines have features and articles on career development often with recommended reading, support groups or associations which could help you.

The library system
There is likely to be at least one library in your town. You can take out books for free or you might just choose to browse. There are books on career development and specific occupations including contact names addresses and phone numbers. In any library, there is also a reference section which contains a mass of career-related information, local, national and international. There may be a photocopier where, for a small charge you can copy contacts for further information. You can also find out about the structure, organisation and personnel of any company from the reference library.

Universities and colleges have reference libraries containing academic texts, journals, reports and professional magazines. There are further specialist libraries located in most major cities. Government departments collate materials which can be looked at by the public.

Information accessed through the library

Government statistics	Extel (financial trends)
Audio data	Consumer publications
Visual data	Encyclopaedias
Private sector reports	Professional publications
Dictionaries	Reference journals

Useful directories accessed through the library

Kelly's Business Directory	Information on over 82,000 industrial, commercial and professional organisations in the UK.
Times 1000 List of Companies	Background information on major companies.
Directory of Grant Making Trusts	List of funds available for research, education and training.

Careers offices
There is a careers office in every major town which offers free advice to young people. For adults there may be a small charge. Careers offices provide guidance on choosing a career. They also have occupational information and can advise on training and funding.

Professional associations
Associations relevant to particular trades and professions provide information to the general public.

TECs
Training and Enterprise Councils exist to provide information and training for businesses.

Local authority
If you require information on your locality, contact your town hall.

Colleges and universities
If you want information on vocational training, you need to contact colleges (further education) or universities (higher education) or the awarding bodies, *eg* City & Guilds.

At work
If you are working, you are surrounded by a mass of information.

The boss
If your line-manager is approachable, you might choose to use them as a potential source of information.

Personnel
If your company has a personnel department, they can be useful for information on internal vacancies and company policy.

Colleagues
Work colleagues in different departments can be a useful mine of information.

Personal
Don't overlook the people within your immediate vicinity as a source of information.

Friends
Friends who are in a similar line of work can be useful. A close friend of mine who works for the Employment Services was initially instrumental in getting me into career development. Those who are not in the same line of work as yourself can offer objective viewpoints which can help refocus.

Family
Even your family might have something to offer. My sister is a Buddhist and she recently recommended to me an excellent book which integrates a spiritual philosophy with good working practices.

WAYS TO GATHER INFORMATION

Now you want to know **how** and **when** to gather the information.

Through a meeting
It's worth while putting aside time to actually meet up with

123 Network Close
Glasgow
0123 456789

White Training
11 Career Road
Brighton

2 May 199X

Dear Mr Turner

As a freelance trainer and specialist in career development, I am currently seeking to expand my horizons.

I have considerable experience working with socially and educationally disadvantaged adults on a variety of life-skills programmes. Further skills include the design and development of training materials.

I understand that you are considering expansion of your freelance training team and wonder if we might meet to discuss possibilities. Please find enclosed a brief professional resumé. I look forward to hearing from you.

Yours sincerely

Laurel Alexander Cert.Ed., AssocIPD

ENC.

Fig. 13. A sample speculative letter.

someone. Sometimes this can be a waste and you can end up feeling frustrated. But when it does work you have the satisfaction of knowing you have laid the basis for any future career networking. You have exchanged information about background, skills and future goals.

Using the telephone

The telephone is an instant and quick way to 'touch base'. If I haven't spoken with my publisher for some time I might give him a quick call which reminds him that I'm still here and he might tell me of any new projects. I recently ended a long-term contract and telephoned someone I used to work for over a year ago. My phone call came at the right time and now I am working for her again delivering a training programme for women.

For fear of sounding like the advert, it's good to talk. By investing in a two-minute phone call, opportunities could open up. You might not get anything concrete from the call, but you remind each other of what you are about and what you are doing, and create a space for potential growth. A few tips:

- Identify what you want to say and who you want to say it to before you call.

- A smile can be 'heard' over the telephone.

- If you want to feel more assertive, stand up when you speak.

By letter

You could write a speculative letter. This type of approach is 'cold calling in writing'. It's a useful approach when looking for work. A few tips:

- Research the companies you want to write to.

- Identify a named individual.

- Ascertain where your skills could fit in.

- Don't ask for a job.

- Get a meeting.

At the end of the day, you are in fact asking for a job, but the rules of the game say you don't ask for a job outright. See the sample letter in Figure 13.

Framework	Example
Define the problem	• I want to earn more money training.
Reduce the problem into workable parts	• Time limit on when I am available for training. • Low pay for the work I am experienced in. • Lack of contacts.
Brainstorm possible solutions	• Make use of the contacts I have got. • Get my local rag once a week and send spec letters to relevant companies. • Go to reference library to find more contacts locally.
Research the workability of the solutions	• Spec letters do work because I have tried with success before. • Existing contacts have brought in work. • Library is a central source of local info.
Interpret and evaluate the data	• Spec letters can go on indefinitely. • Spec letters might not bring in work now but I can build up my contacts. • I could use existing contacts to make more contacts. • Library can help identify local market for training.
Select and implement a solution	• Will get the local rag and write spec letters even when I have enough work. • Will go to reference library. • Will keep in regular touch with existing contacts.
Evaluate the implemented solution	• Ongoing.

Fig. 14. Problem-solving framework.

Social interaction

You might network accidentally or deliberately through social interaction. It might be a social event linked to work or it might be a personal social event. Developing your **conversational skills** will help you to blend career networking with pleasure. People like to talk about themselves. Conversation is easier when you ask other people questions. It gives you some space and time to assess the situation and where you fit in. Be careful not to do all the listening. Involve yourself in self-disclosure as well. Stimulating and useful conversation is about give and take.

- *Opening gambits* might include:

  'Hello. I'm Richard Redgrave.' (*Introducing yourself.*)

  'What line of work are you in?' (*Basic information exchange.*)

  'I see Carol is preparing for her speech. What do you think she might say?' (*Comment followed by question.*)

  'What do you think of the new white paper on education?' (*Bring in a topical subject.*)

  'I've been speaking to Ken about the possibilities of promotion.' (*Self-disclosure.*)

  'I found your report on bee hives most stimulating. How did you do your research?' (*Compliment followed by question.*)

- *Permissions to talk* might include:

  'Is there something on your mind?'

  'I'd like to hear your viewpoint.'

- *Continuation expression* might include:

  'Go on, I see.'

  'Right.'

  'Tell me more.'

  'Please continue.'

SOLVING PROBLEMS

Effective thinking skills contribute to how we gather and use information. Problem-solving skills form a framework for clear thinking which in turn can produce constructive action. (See the framework in Figure 14.)

CONCLUSION

Gathering and imparting information can be as creative as you like. As you build upon your career networking skills you can begin to identify more unusual ways to get yourself seen, heard and noticed.

CASE STUDIES

Carol's getting retrained

Carol wants occupational information and advice on getting retrained. Her husband has provided her with some insight into the role of computers in business but she feels she needs some impartial guidance. She is considering her local further education college and some other private secretarial colleges in the area. Another idea she has is to go into employment agencies to see what types of software are the most popular with the employers in her area.

John's entitled to free help

John needs to look at his jobsearch skills and as he is claiming benefit, he is entitled to participate in a free workshop to improve his techniques.

Iris wants to expand her horizons

Iris would like to transfer her life-skills training to another occupation. She is ready for a new challenge and is prepared to go to a private careers counsellor for some guidance.

DISCUSSION POINTS

1. Analyse how thinking, feeling and action interact.

2. How does taking responsibility or 'personal ownership' affect your thinking skills?

3. What is meant by the term 'information society'?

7
Getting Yourself Noticed

Career networking means raising your visibility. Whether you are looking to be employed, are seeking promotion or want to increase your market share as a self-employed person, you need to be seen as an expert. We have looked at the basic methods of getting yourself known. Here we look at the more unusual.

NETWORKING BY TECHNOLOGY

A whole new jargon has sprung up – the Web, Internet, e-mail. The good old-fashioned post has been dubbed 'the snail-mail' because, compared to technology, it's so slow.

The Internet
The World Wide Web (based on the Internet) is a method of communicating from computer to computer (across different types of computers) at low cost. Thousands of people across the world access the Web every day. Readers can access the Web and browse through a variety of information on 'web-sites'. They then contact advertisers using e-mail.

The Open University recruiting on the Internet
1995 saw the Open University using the Internet for the first time to recruit over thirty academic staff specialising in technology. They used a mixture of traditional methods and new technology to advertise the vacancies including details of the post on the World Wide Web. During the three-week application period, the Open University's Web page was accessed more than 10,000 times. They received 1,000 requests for application forms by e-mail while a further 1,600 applied by phone and post. The popular method of receiving the application form and other particulars was by e-mail. Almost 16 per cent of all applicants saw the vacancies on the Web.

The intranet

There is now a re-application of this form of communication to an internal networking system called an intranet. This is a network of computers operating in multi-media form available to the internal staff of an organisation. Companies such as the BBC, Ford, Olivetti and Mobil have allowed this process to occur already. The data most commonly accessed is internal vacancies. employment conditions and social information. This facility is likely to be expanded to low-cost international conferencing and communication with customers and suppliers.

Using fax

I've recently acquired a fax machine and it has improved my relations with magazine editors because I can write an article in the morning and it is on their desk in the afternoon. When I was negotiating a new book with my publisher, he wanted the chapter headings rewritten. I rewrote them and he had them three hours later. The author's agreement came shortly after. The fax puts you right there − making contact instantly.

Project: the Internet
Use your local library to find out where you can have public access to the Internet in action.

CONSIDERING ALTERNATIVES

If you have the confidence, there are a number of further alternatives you might consider incorporating into your career networking programme.

Participating in an exhibition

Most trades and professions have exhibitions. There are two types of categories: trade shows which attract commercial buyers and consumer shows for the general public. When considering this option. Ask yourself:

- What are my objectives?
- Can I afford the cost of the stand?
- What literature will I offer?

- What will I display on the stand?
- Who will man the stand?

> **Project**
> If you are in business for yourself or you have a specific trade or profession, find out from your local library what types of exhibitions you could visit.

Creating a team of like-minded people

You might consider organising an advisory body of experts. Or you could enrol supporters of a cause in a special interest group so that you can bring power to bear on others. If you are seeking promotion, you might get together with people to improve crèche facilities or to develop a more effective way of completing a job. Decision-makers like to see pro-active people who take the initiative. If you run your own business, you might want to create a pressure group, especially if your company is involved in providing a service or product which affects the community or the environment.

Holding a seminar

Holding a seminar would bring you to the attention of others. If you are running your own business, you might hold a free seminar with refreshments. If you are networking for promotion, invite influential people along, arrange some guest speakers including yourself and deliver an event around forward thinking in the area you wish to get into.

> **Project: attending a seminar**
> If you are a member of an association, have you read the latest literature to see if there is a seminar or meeting? Have you attended any yet? If you haven't, make sure you get along to something during the next three months.

Having a party

If you've got something to celebrate, why not throw a party and expand your contacts?

Project: have a party
Get your friends together and ask each of them to bring one guest. Network the room and get to know everyone.

Writing a newsletter

If you work for yourself, writing an occasional newsletter is a good way of keeping your clients informed of past and current successes and informing them of future products or services. If you work for a company, why not start up a newsletter for staff, clients or customers?

Writing an article

If you write an article, you could put your professional details at the end which could bring in enquiries. Writing articles for the company magazine might bring you to the attention of the people who matter.

Project: write an article
See if you can write 1,000 words on something you are passionate about. Then try to write 1,000 words on some aspect of your profession or trade. Give both to a friend to read.

Writing a book

Writing a practical, non-fiction book raises your profile and gives a professional message that you are an expert in your field. If seeking promotion, you could give the decision-maker a complimentary copy! When writing your CV, put down your achievements as an author – it might open doors. As a trainer in career development, I am helping to build my credibility by writing this book.

Issuing a press release

A press release is an excellent opportunity to get free publicity for yourself. If you run your own business and are sponsoring a football team, have discovered something incredible, given money to the local cats home or have something else equally newsworthy, a press release is a freebie way of letting the public know your name and how wonderful you are.

Using the radio

This is where members of the public phone in with their queries and you as the spokesperson answer them. An example would be if you had a business as a travel agency. Get involved in a radio phone-in providing solutions to people's holidays questions or offer advice through an interview, especially if there is something topical you could relate to in the news.

Using direct mail

If you are self-employed. direct mail is a powerful way of targeting potential customers.

14 steps for a successful direct mail campaign
1. Research your idea.
2. Understand your customers.
3. Test your market.
4. Review your competitors' direct mail approach.
5. Decide on your budget.
6. Construct your offer.
7. Set a schedule for completion.
8. Develop your package.
9. Acquire the mailing list.
10. Write the copy and create the artwork.
11. Get print quotes.
12. Print your package.
13. Prepare for mailing.
14. Evaluate response.

GAINING PUBLIC SPEAKING SKILLS

Public speaking is a crucial part of career networking inasmuch as it raises your profile as an expert. You are on a 'platform' demonstrating your expertise. If you are well qualified and have a track record of practical experience, there is no reason why you shouldn't add public speaking to your toolbox of networking skills. Public speaking establishes you as an authority in your field and brings you to the notice of a wider network.

The first secret of public speaking is to work out **what** you want to say, **why** you want to say it, to **whom** and **how**?

Objective checklist
● What do I want my audience to know?

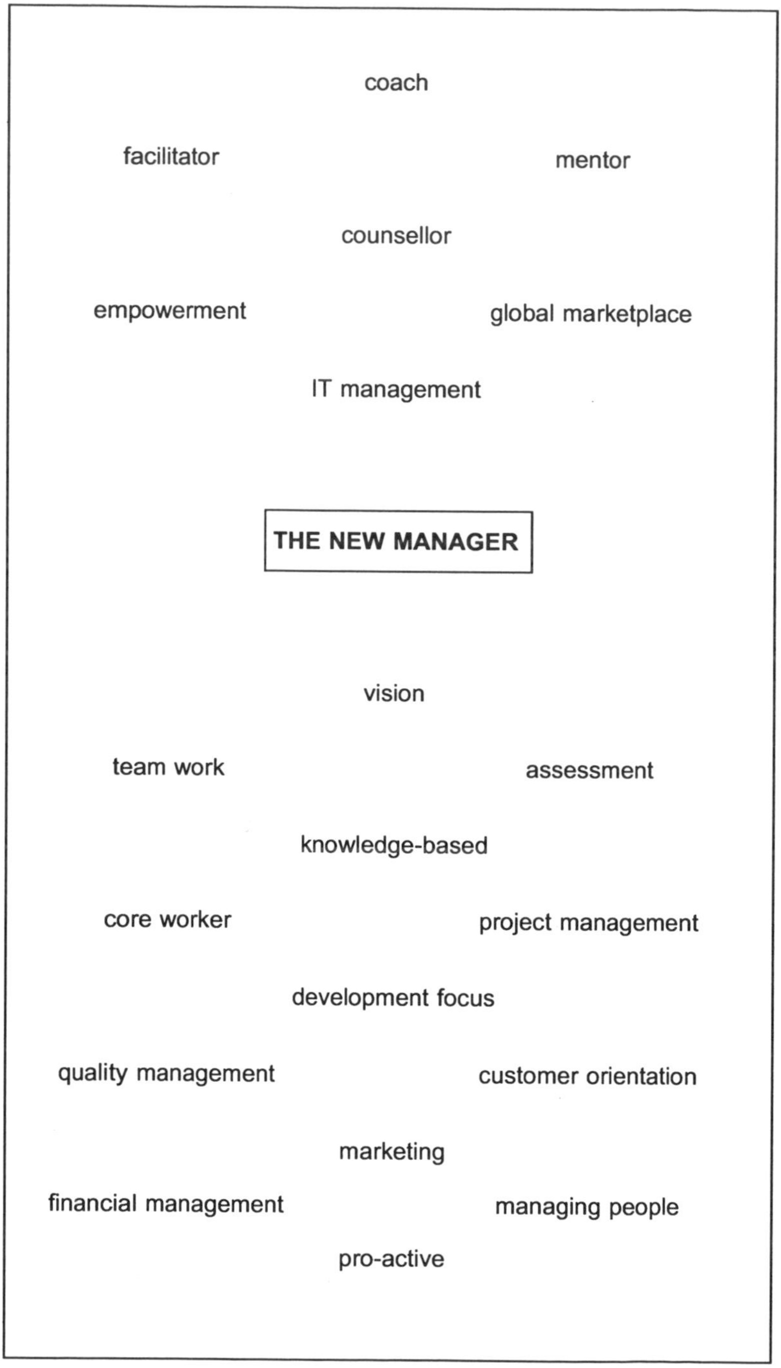

coach

facilitator   mentor

counsellor

empowerment   global marketplace

IT management

THE NEW MANAGER

vision

team work   assessment

knowledge-based

core worker   project management

development focus

quality management   customer orientation

marketing

financial management   managing people

pro-active

Fig. 15. Spider web of ideas for speech on the new manager.

- What do I want them to go away with?
- How do I want to come across to them?

Audience checklist
- How many people will there be?
- What are their ages?
- What is their background?
- Are the refreshments before or after my delivery?

Facility checklist
- Is there a rostrum?
- What is the amplification?
- How long am I speaking for?
- Am I going to use visual aids?

Now comes the **speech preparation**. Let us say that you want to speak for thirty minutes on *the New Manager*. You might want to do a **spider web** of ideas as suggested in Figure 15.

You then need to put the thoughts in some sort of **logical order**, demonstrating them with current quotes, examples or statistics. Keep asking yourself 'Will this be of interest to the listeners – why should they keep listening?' Consider the motivations of your audience. Always start with something topical. Following through from the above example, your outline might be something like this:

The changing face of this company	Implementation of core workers, joke about working overtime
Key qualities of the core worker as manager	Vision, project management, development focus, pro-active, examples of key workers
Customer orientation and marketing to their needs	Example of existing clients and possible new clients, how we are spreading out to the global marketplace

Quality management	How we are monitoring and improving standards, mention Dave's role here
People management	Empowerment, facilitator, mentor, counsellor, team work, the manager as coach and assessor, importance of seeing the workers as key to the success of the company
Additional roles	IT and financial management
Wrap up	Asking the audience to look at their own skills and self-development as managers.

Delivering your speech

When you actually deliver, you need to quickly state your purpose and use the time to inform and persuade. Identify yourself as one of the audience. If you make a mistake, see it from the audience's point of view and use it. Involve your audience and make them feel as if they are the most important people in your life at that moment. Establish a rapport by showing your understanding of their situation.

Never be boring. Aim for vocal variety through emphasis. Use words that are right for you but also aim for the emotions of your listeners. Identify a common use of language. Don't pitch over or under your listener. Use laughter early on if possible. Get attention quickly and be enthusiastic. Keep your sentences short and simple. Keep your words relevant!

Make sure you are breathing deeply and smoothly from the stomach to promote relaxation and to make your voice carry well. Be aware of using positive and open body language which encourages your audience to look at you and listen.

Using visual aids is a good idea. Amongst the best to use are flipcharts, overhead projector, slides or a video.

Aim for smooth transitions between different parts of your delivery. Make sure you have a strong ending with summary points to remind your listeners of the key points. Prepare for questions.

USING THE MEDIA

A press release

A press release needs to have a sense of urgency about it and needs to be topical. The immediate questions it must answer should be:

Prepare	Never be boring
Make your fear work for you	State your purpose
Analyse your audience	Inform and persuade
Get feedback	Get vocal variety
Aim for variety through emphasis	Breathe correctly
Involve your audience	Be one of the audience
Use words that are right for you	Aim for the emotions
Use positive body language	Use laughter early on
Get attention quickly	Build on your strengths
Use visual aids	Be enthusiastic
Make smooth transitions	Establish a rapport
Make a strong ending	Prepare for questions

Fig. 16. The public speaking checklist.

- Who?
- What?
- When?
- How?
- Why?
- Where?

The release should be no longer than two pages of A4, double spaced, with a grabbing headline. If you include a photograph, make sure it has an explanatory caption. Include a contact name, phone and fax number.

Radio

If you are considering using the radio to establish your expertise thereby increasing your career networking contacts, you need to have a lively voice that sounds enthusiastic. Throw in humour, topical facts and subject knowledge and you will be listened to. There are many more radio stations than TV stations in Britain and most of them are always on the lookout for items of interest. The best contacts in radio are the researchers. Names can be obtained from TV magazines, credits after the programmes or by contacting the station direct.

CONCLUSION

Career networking is as creative as you want it to be. But you need to be clear about why you are networking and what you want from it. Do you want a job? Do you want promotion? Do you want more customers or clients?

Networking is getting to know people and opening yourself up so that other people can get to know you. However, you may be in a position where you have been made redundant or maybe you haven't worked for some time. In which case, your people skills are likely to be a bit rusty. You may feel you have lost touch with people. So how do you begin getting back? What can you do to get a sense of belonging which might lead to a lucrative job offer? We explore these questions in the next chapter.

CASE STUDIES

Carol's got the right byte
Because of her husband's work as a computer consultant, Carol is aware of the Internet and its potential for networking.

John needs to make contact
John tends to keep himself to himself. His people skills are limited because he feels more comfortable with things than with people.

Iris has her fax right
Iris has a fax in her office at home and uses it to make regular contact with training agencies who provide her with work. She is in the process of writing a book on customer care which is an area she does NVQ assessment for.

DISCUSSION POINTS

1. Look through a newspaper or trade magazine and analyse what makes an advert stand out.

2. How does Richard Branson influence the image of his companies?

3. What are the ways you might consider to raise your professional profile?

8
Networking While Unemployed

If you have been out of work you are probably aware of how difficult it can be to maintain momentum. You lose contact with work colleagues, you may lose touch with current trends in your profession or trade and your jobsearch skills are rusty. It is at this time that you need to make a conscious effort to improve your career networking skills in order to move forward and find work. Did you know 30 per cent of vacancies are filled through:

- newspapers
- trade magazines
- Jobcentres
- agencies
- on-site cold calling
- TV
- radio
- shop windows?

Did you know 70 per cent of vacancies are filled through:

- word of mouth
- a speculative approach
- past workmates?

BEING MADE REDUNDANT

Redundancy might have come like a bolt out of the blue or you may have heard rumours for weeks. It is important to realise that it is the job, not the person, that has been made redundant. When redundancy first hits, you need to bear in mind the following:

- Make sure of your redundancy package.
- Check with the Jobcentre about any benefits you may be entitled to.

- Take time out to think.

- Identify your existing skills.

- Find out about growth industries.

- Ask yourself if you want to stay in the same line of work.

- Ask yourself if you would like to change career direction.

- Ask yourself if you would like to become self employed.

- Enquire about retraining.

- Research funding possibilities.

- Prepare a current CV.

- Improve your interview techniques.

- **Develop your career networking skills.**

Networking before you leave

As soon as you know that you will be leaving, begin networking with anyone who can help you. Suppliers, clients, line-managers, personnel, other work colleagues, any associations you might belong to. Use where you are to put the feelers out for work leads.

Starting up a redundancy network

You might consider getting together with other colleagues who are being made redundant to help and support each other. If you can form a group of half a dozen people, then you can get onto each other's networks and increase your chances of locating opportunities.

Project: networking for job leads
Get a plan of your organisational structure. Pinpoint who might help you with job leads.

USING EMPLOYMENT SERVICES

Employment Services (ES) is part of the Civil Service and is the country's largest employment organisation. ES runs Jobcentres which can be found in almost every town. You will have a Client Advisor who can assist with:

- places on free courses for those returning to work or seeking to upgrade their jobsearch skills
- costs of travelling to interviews
- membership of jobclubs for networking, support and access to stationery
- direct access to jobs
- opportunities for you to try out jobs before committing yourself
- benefit advice and rebates.

When you make your first appointment to go to a Jobcentre, you will need to take your P45, your National Insurance number and your partner's National Insurance number if you wish to claim for an adult dependant.

Jobsearch Plus

If you have been unemployed for three months, you could go on a free three-day workshop called Jobsearch Plus, which offers guidance on the local labour market, how to write a CV and how to make speculative approaches.

Jobclubs

You can join a jobclub after being unemployed for six months. You have access to local and national newspapers, trade journals, word processing equipment, photocopiers and postage. There is also guidance on CV writing and interview techniques. This really is one of the best ways of getting back into the networking swing.

There are two types of jobclub – the Standard which is for most people and the Executive which is for professional people.

DEA

DEA stands for Disability Employment Advisor. If you have a disability (physical, mental distress, drink or drug related), the DEA will help you target the sort of job that suits you. The DEA is part of the Placing, Assessment and Counselling Team (PACT) which provides specialist advice to disabled people and their employers.

USING EMPLOYMENT AGENCIES

Employment agencies do not charge for their services. They exist to help you find work. There are specialist agencies, *eg* for nurses, accountants or computer personnel. Most agencies have a permanent and a temporary section. Charges are made to the employer and not to yourself. Beware of being asked for money either in advance or if successfully placed in work. This is unethical.

Project: agencies
Look through the *Yellow Pages* and make a list of the agencies suitable for you to visit.

USING THE TECs

The Training and Enterprise Councils provide funding and access to a broad range of programmes including:

- career guidance
- Training for Work (helping the unemployed find jobs and achieve qualifications)
- Learning for Work (helping the unemployed to pursue full-time vocational studies).

USING CAREER COUNSELLING

This is a growing area of business where you *will* be charged for the service provided. There are both general and specific areas of counselling, *eg* women, redundancy, those coming up to retirement. Career counselling:

- tells you about working environments
- may suggest possible contacts
- tells you what kind of jobs match your skills, needs and experience
- defines what skills are needed for a particular job
- recommends additional training to give credibility
- may uncover different areas of employment you hadn't considered
- will challenge you to think more creatively.

USING THE CAREERS OFFICE

There are career centres in most large towns and they provide information on local employment opportunities, career descriptions, information on what skills are needed for a particular job and information on training and educational opportunities. They are primarily aimed at younger people.

GETTING JOB LEADS

Career networking is about making contact for information. In this day of fluctuating work opportunities, you need to be constantly networking for job leads, even when working.

Newspapers
Consider the local and national press. Even if you don't see a vacancy that suits you, use the contact name to make a speculative approach. The national press has certain job-types advertised on specific days (see Figure 17).

Journals
If you belong to a professional association, you probably receive a journal. If there is a situations vacant section, either apply for suitable work or send a speculative letter in.

Ceefax
Vacancies are often advertised through Ceefax. Use the TV in the same way as you would the press.

Getting onto computer networks
There is a new growth arm in recruiting whereby your name and occupational details are inserted onto a candidate database which is available to thousands of potential employers in the UK and abroad via their desk-top terminals.

Sending speculative letters
This is a powerful way of accessing contacts, information or even a job, see Chapter 6.

Project: speculative letters
Research the companies which might have the type of work you're looking for. Send out six speculative letters a week.

Appointments	Newspaper	Day
Art/communication	*Guardian*	Monday/Thursday
	Daily Telegraph	Monday
	Independent	Wednesday/Friday
	Daily Express	Tuesday
	Times	Wednesday
Teaching	*Daily Telegraph*	Thursday
	Guardian	Tuesday
	Independent	Thursday
	Daily Express	Tuesday/Thursday
	Times	Monday
Financial	*Daily Telegraph*	Monday
	Guardian	Thursday
	Independent	Tuesday
	Financial Times	Wednesday/Thursday
	Daily Mail	Wednesday
	Times	Thursday
Civil Service	*Daily Telegraph*	Monday
	Guardian	Wednesday/Friday
	Independent	Thursday
	Daily Mail	Wednesday
	Daily Express	Tuesday
	Times	Thursday
Information Technology	*Daily Telegraph*	Monday
	Guardian	Thursday
	Independent	Monday
	Daily Mail	Thursday
	Daily Express	Thursday
	Times	Tuesday
Engineers	*Daily Telegraph*	Tuesday/Thursday
	Guardian	Thursday
	Independent	Monday
	Daily Mail	Thursday
	Daily Express	Monday/Tuesday
	Times	Thursday

Fig. 17. National newspaper appointments days.

Appointments	Newspaper	Day
Secretarial	Daily Mail	Tuesday
	Daily Express	Tuesday
	Times	Monday/Tuesday/Wednesday
Management	Daily Telegraph	Tuesday/Thursday/Saturday
	Guardian	Monday/Wednesday/Thursday
	Independent	Thursday/Sunday
	Financial Times	Wednesday
	Daily Mail	Thursday
	Daily Express	Monday/Wednesday/Thursday
	Times	Thursday
Science	Daily Telegraph	Monday/Thursday
	Guardian	Thursday
	Independent	Monday
	Daily Mail	Thursday
	Daily Express	Thursday
	Times	Thursday
Sales and Marketing	Daily Telegraph	Wednesday/Thursday
	Guardian	Monday/Thursday
	Independent	Wednesday
	Financial Times	Wednesday
	Daily Mail	Tuesday/Thursday
	Daily Express	Wednesday
	Times	Thursday
Works Management	Daily Telegraph	Thursday
	Guardian	Monday
	Independent	Monday/Thursday
	Daily Mail	Thursday
	Daily Express	Thursday
	Times	Thursday

Fig. 17. Contd.

Socialising

Down the pub, at a party or a meeting over lunch could all provide opportunities to network and exchange information which could lead to work.

Cold-calling

Some work can be got just from walking in off the street. The construction industry, for example, gets most of its workers this way. The first job I ever got was because I had bunked off school, saw a job for a window dresser in a fashion shop and walked in off the street to ask for it.

RETURNING TO STUDY

You might consider returning to education or training as part of your jobsearch strategy. To begin the process, you might need to network with the careers office, colleges and universities. Issues to consider might include the following:

- Do you want to return full- or part-time?

- What are the costs, *eg* course fees, exam fees, books and equipment, travel and childcare?

- Do you want a confidence-building course to prepare you for paid work?

- Do you want a qualification course for a new job?

- Do you want a course for updating skills in your current profession?

- Do you want a course to help you set up in self-employment?

Using computer-aided guidance

Jobcentres and libraries have computer-aided guidance for TAPS (Training Access Points) giving information about training both locally and nationally.

Training for work

This is a scheme initiated by the government which offers free training to an NVQ (National Vocational Qualification) standard in subjects such as information technology, care, sports and leisure, and business administration. Work experience is usually part of the scheme. Contact your local Jobcentre to find out more.

Further education
Colleges offer a wide range of vocational training to young and mature students. If you are on benefit you need to be careful about the number of hours you study for. At the time of writing this book, if you study for more than 16 hours per week, your benefit will be affected. Full- and part-time courses are available to NVQ, certificate and diploma standard. Subjects include beauty, community care, construction, engineering and health. You can find out about funding from Jobcentres, careers offices or the colleges themselves.

Higher education
You might be interested in taking a degree at university, but may not have the necessary qualifications to get onto a course. Taking an **Access course** will provide you with a way in. Access courses are run by further and higher education institutions. They are part-time and one year in length and are designed to provide, to mature students especially, study skills plus a basic grounding in a relevant study. They also offer a good networking opportunity. You would be meeting people who are considering returning to study and who have probably been out of work for some time. You would also be networking with educational institutions which could provide you with more insight into the wider courses on offer.

Using open learning
If you are housebound, living in a rural area, looking after children or a dependant, you might want to explore the possibility of distance or open learning. Using this method, you study at home, in your own time and at your own pace. You would be allocated a personal tutor who sets you work and marks your assignments. Additional methods may be using the TV (Open University), video or audio tapes, or attending summer schools or weekend seminars.

Project: returning to study
Go to your local library or contact the relevant colleges and universities and get their prospectuses.

USING THE INTERVIEW

The interview situation is one which offers you scope. It is tempting when preparing for and undergoing an interview to give away your

Preparation for interview

Research the company (*eg* size – what do they do)

Research the job

(*eg* description and purpose of job – responsibilities)

Assess your relevant skills, strengths and experience

Improve your communication skills

Prepare for their questions

Prepare your questions

Interviews in action

Don't rubbish past employers

Provide evidence of what you have done

Provide evidence of what you can do

Don't speak for more than 30 seconds without pausing

Watch for the interviewer's reactions

Look interested

Concentrate

Volunteer appropriate information

Give simple answers to questions

Be positive

Avoid the words 'only' and 'just'

Smile

Fig. 18. The successful interview toolkit.

power. People tend to behave as though the potential employer has all the power. Admittedly, they can say yes or no to us, but equally so can we to them. The interview is your opportunity to tell someone about yourself but also to get information about their company or about any other relevant work-related lead. (See Figure 18.)

RESEARCHING A PROSPECTIVE EMPLOYER

You can access the latest accounts and other financial information plus director names from the Registrar of Companies and Limited Partnerships. Your local Chamber of Commerce may also be able to help.

IDENTIFYING YOUR GOALS

Ask yourself the following questions:

• What are my career goals for the next six months?

• Who can I get to help me achieve these goals?

• How can they help me achieve these goals?

CONCLUSION

Career networking is a constant process. We network when we are out of work and we network when we are in work. By consolidating and extending our network, we build bridges for the future, so that when we are in work but are seeking to expand our horizons, we can take advantage of our contacts. Networking in work is the next step.

CASE STUDIES

Carol's networking with her tutor
As Carol becomes more experienced with computers and learns more about business administration at college, she is using her tutors to bounce ideas around about finding work.

John's going for a career change
John is claiming benefit and volunteered to go on a three-day workshop suggested to him by his claimant advisor at the Jobcentre, to brush up on his jobsearch techniques. He was given

more information on being retrained and is now considering a career change and going into betting shop management.

Iris is building on her qualifications

Iris is contemplating going into the field of counselling with a view to specialising. She has already taken a one-year part-time certificate in counselling and now needs to get the diploma which would be another two years part-time study. She could study alongside her training work.

DISCUSSION POINTS

1. Do you think it is a good idea to have specific occupational networks for people who have been made redundant? If so why?

2. Some people place adverts in the media, detailing the type of work they're looking for. What are the pros and cons of this way of networking for work?

3. If you wanted to study from home, how would you build up your network of support?

9
Networking in Work

Career networking while in work has a different emphasis. If you work for an employer, you might want to network for promotion or to improve your skills-base. You might want to network to prepare for redundancy or you might want to form a pressure group. You may just have received promotion in which case you will want to network to get to know your colleagues and the job.

If you work for yourself, you will want to network with suppliers, colleagues in similar trades or professions, the media (for publicity purposes) and customers and clients.

This chapter looks at the situations and skills necessary to network, whether you work for someone else or for yourself.

MAKING EFFECTIVE PRESENTATIONS

If you work for yourself, you may regularly be in the position of having to present your product or service to other professionals or to the public. If you work for a company, making presentations may be part of your remit. Either situation can provide you with a good platform from which you can branch out and network. (See Figure 19.)

Improving your appearance
When standing up to give a presentation, button up your jacket. A tie is to a man what earrings are to a woman – they both draw attention to the face which is what you want. Avoid bulging pockets and fussy detail in your clothing.

Improving your voice
Practise reading out loud (maybe recording your voice on tape) to see how you sound. Develop expression in your voice and improve your pronunciation, pace and modulation.

PREPARATION

Set your objective   Identify your audience

Decide on location

Get a good opening   Include questions   Simplify text

Ensure content is relevant   Keep sections short

Get the audience involved

Include various methods of presenting

Decide when you are going to answer questions

VERBAL DELIVERY

Pitch language at the right   Use the first or
level   second person

Keep main point of   Use examples often
sentence near beginning

Keep audience involved

If asked a difficult question, throw it open to the audience

USING VISUAL AIDS

Don't stand in front   Keep leads well out of
of the visual aids   tripping-over way

Use visuals when attention span is low

Don't turn your back on the audience

Switch off machinery   Know where the
when you have finished   on/off switches are

Fig. 19. Action checklist for making presentations.

Lowering your stress levels

Practise relaxation techniques, especially deep breathing exercises. Doing some physical exercise before you present will move the adrenaline through your muscles, releasing them into action rather than freezing them into paralysis.

Making a formal presentation

Avoid holding your hands behind your back or crossing your arms. Keep your body open and make natural hand movements with the palms up. Avoid pointing fingers or making a steeple with your hands. Smile occasionally, make good eye contact and end declarations in a low tone.

Speaking to a large audience

Project your voice and let all of you be seen. If you are at a podium, make sure your face down to your chest is seen. Don't spend any longer than 10 minutes delivering a formally prepared speech. Wear something red to inspire confidence.

Making an informal presentation

Draw out discussion by encouraging questions. Move around more – even sit down occasionally. Make sure you actively listen, make good eye contact and nod your head to show understanding. Facilitate debate and exchange. You might want to take notes.

MASTERING MEETINGS

Any meeting gives you a fantastic opportunity to increase your visibility as a powerful and knowledgeable communicator.

Your preparation for the meeting should cover:

- familiarity with the minutes of the last meeting (or several)

- familiarity with the group attendees

- study of the agenda and any relevant handouts

- knowledge of the seating arrangement and any 'territorial' stamps

- preparation of specific ideas for agenda items that interest you (if you're planning to launch an idea, test the waters before the meeting with a key decision-maker).

able	advantage	brilliant
confidence	controlled	detail
economical	effective	emphasis
now	outstanding	professional
volume	tremendous	top
today	money-making	lowest cost
latest	key	instant
impelling	immediate	help
quality	quickly	results
satisfaction	smart	solved
special	successful	expert
excited	fair	new
save	safety	evaluate
proven	discover	guarantee
results	you	update
complete	endorsed	maximise
image	value	inform
sure	best	personal
affect	future	venture
customer	skills	empower
practical	valid	facilitate
knowledge	fast	reliable
original	motivate	involve
measure		

Fig. 20. Key words to use in meetings and presentations.

During the meeting:

- Sit where you can be seen and heard (near to the head or to the right of someone with power).

- If you anticipate conflict, sit on that person's dominant side so that they will feel less threatened.

- If you are new, ask people to introduce themselves.

- Speak up at least once.

- Don't allow an argument to turn into a battle.

- If you want to exert an influence, speak early in a discussion.

- Use powerful mannerisms.

- Speak with authority.

- Use powerful and effective words (see Figure 20).

Increasing your meeting power

As a participant
When you have found what the objectives of the meeting are, prepare to be supportive and encouraging. Aim to earn authority as a leader among equals. Be resourceful and collaborate on objectives. Participate and become involved. Take on responsibility and visibility.

Chairing the meeting
Ascertain whether a meeting is really necessary or whether you could meet your objectives through another means. Try to meet in the morning. Include only those who are essential and can make a contribution. Supply everyone with an agenda – get the facts out. Have someone to take minutes and send them out within 24 hours of the meeting ending. Generate discussion leading to proposed solutions. Evaluate the pros and cons of solutions and gain agreement on the best.

Seating
To gain recognition, sit within good eye contact of decision-makers. If presenting, arrive early and select your vantage point. If it is a long table, choose the middle of one side. If it is an oval table, choose one of the narrow curved ends.

To mitigate a confrontation, sit next to the challenger. To avoid attention, sit in a blind spot for the Chair and wear a neutral outfit with no accessories.

Body language
Undermining signals include slouching in your chair, looking down at your notes, out of the window or up at the ceiling, turning away, folding arms across the body, using closed, threatening gestures and a deadpan or cynical expression.

Positive signals include sitting upright and alert, sitting forward, keeping your eyes on the speaker, taking notes on key points, turning body to speaker, opening your body language and smiling.

BEING VIEWED AS A TEAM MEMBER

The growing trend in business is towards teamwork. As companies are becoming more streamlined and smaller, there is a leaning towards working on specific projects in teams. The teams may not always work together and the members may be of different cultures, background and expertise.

Effective networking is teamwork. When we career network, we are touching base with people with whom we can exchange information in order to work towards skills improvement or promotion. Teamwork at work is similar. We work together for a common aim, each bringing specific skills and knowledge.

What are you like as a team member?
In the groups of statements below, tick the one which you think describes you most accurately. Then read the descriptions of types of team player which follow:

(a) I view the team as important.
(b) I take a problem-solving approach to tasks.
(c) I am forceful.
(d) I am enthusiastic.

(a) I like a relaxed atmosphere.
(b) I am a slow decision maker.
(c) I am impatient.
(d) I need social recognition.

(a) I like to identify with the Company.
(b) I am conscientious.
(c) I like prestige.
(d) I am sympathetic.

(a) I am patient.   (b) I am conventional.
(c) I am easily bored.   (d) I am good at persuading
                                         others.

(a) I am predictable.   (b) I am a worrier.
(c) I enjoy taking risks.   (d) I am impulsive.

(a) I am uncomfortable with   (b) I have high standards.
    change.
(c) I need to win.   (d) I am friendly.

(a) I prefer close relationships.   (b) I like established procedures.
(c) I don't like to be controlled.   (d) I am intuitive.

Mostly (a)s indicates a TRADITIONAL teamplayer
As a traditional teamplayer, you like to know where you stand. You
are very much orientated towards working with others and need to
identify with a cause. You are motivated by insecurity and a need to
belong.

Mostly (b)s indicates an ANALYTICAL teamplayer
If you came out as an analytical teamplayer, you like to stick to the
rules. You identify with facts and figures – emotional content makes
you uneasy. Most likely you are a perfectionist.

Mostly (c)s indicates a DOMINATING teamplayer
As a dominating teamplayer you would make a good leader. You
are competitive and motivated by a need to be in control.

Mostly (d)s indicates a CHARISMATIC teamplayer
A charismatic teamplayer, is a salesperson. You are likely to be
quite emotional and insecure. You may tend to see yourself through
the eyes of others.

USING APPRAISALS

Broadly speaking there are three types of appraisal:

• for promotion
• team-building
• performance.

An appraisal:

- helps develop personal potential
- gives an opportunity to criticise upwards
- develops potential to meet future organisational requirements
- evaluates present performance against agreed objectives.

Successful appraisals
Getting the most out of appraisals involves giving and receiving of constructive criticism. Some tips to help you include:

- Be specific when giving criticism, *eg* 'l didn't feel you gave me any acknowledgement following completion of the project'.
- Avoid stereotyping, *eg* 'You're a typical manager'.
- Focus on behaviour not the whole person, *eg* 'Over the past two months. you have given me more work than I can cope with'.
- Acknowledge the positive, *eg* 'I think that you are an observant person but I'm not sure you understand this particular situation'.
- Keep to the point.

When you are being criticised, you don't have to agree with it. You might choose to agree in part, *eg* 'I agree my time-keeping has not been very good the last two weeks, but normally I am on time.' There need be no shame in agreeing in full to a criticism. This doesn't mean that you are a bad person, only that a particular aspect of your behaviour has the potential to be better. Another technique which demonstrates your confidence is to invite criticism, *eg* 'What did you think of the work I did on the Wilson project?'

MOVING UP TO MANAGEMENT

If you wish to move into management, you need to prepare the ground well.

Organisational politics
Organisational politics may be defined as:

- personal networks
- behind the scenes decision-making

- formal authority

- bureaucratic empire-building

- specific and expert knowledge

- control of technology

- control of the purse strings.

Self-doubt can hold us back from management. We may think that we lack commitment or we can't cope with pressure. We might downgrade our skills thinking that we lack organisational skills or can't make decisions.

We could choose to believe that our skills are being enhanced all the time, that our experiences count, that our capabilities are making a positive difference and contribute to the organisational growth and that our achievements are important.

Management skills

Management can be viewed as a multifaceted activity which involves specific skills and characteristics.

Workplace management characteristics and skills

valuing others	managing meetings	time management
loyalty to staff	approachability	fairness
being pro-active	challenging yourself	being human
admitting your	being focused	being creative
mistakes	taking risks	showing courage
self-expression	being unique	adaptability
co-operation	innovation	resourcefulness
confidence	decisiveness	objectivity
selection and	skills training	interpersonal skills
recruitment	dealing with conflict	administering
doing appraisals	consulting with	discipline
giving feedback	others	providing energy
giving encourage-	coaching	counselling
ment	motivating others	strategic planning
facilitating change	clarifying expecta-	managing resources
setting objectives	tions	listening
quality management	decision-making	working in teams
taking action	prioritising	

Be courteous	Allow others to develop
Make yourself available	Be positive
Value others	Express yourself
Treat other people as human	Clarify your expectations
Listen to others	Provide direction
Take genuine interest in others	Give feedback
Provide direction	Have vision
Ask others for their opinions	Be fair
Practise what you preach	Take the initiative
Admit your mistakes	Plan with others
Encourage others	Remain calm
Praise achievement	Take risks
Be loyal	Be trustworthy

Fig. 21. Some of the best ways to manage people.

Future management skills
According to Skills and Enterprise Network, the skills a manager will be required to have include:

- a working knowledge of the global market
- coaching
- project management
- counselling
- staff development
- team building
- IT management
- languages
- customer service
- managing change
- leading others
- assessing.

Networking for management
- Get a mentor.
- Develop job-specific skills.
- Gain more knowledge.
- Be seen as an expert.
- Join a professional organisation.
- Have a vision and be passionate about that vision.
- Show integrity.
- Join the social network of your company.

Management styles
Are you:

- *The supporter*
  helpful   patient   likeable   easygoing   agreeable

- *The motivator*
  dramatic social   enthusiastic   charismatic   chatterbox

- *The perfectionist*
  orderly   accurate   reserved   self-disciplined   fretful

- *The director*
  forceful   risk-taker   powerful   organiser   ambitious

BUSINESS WRITING

Much networking is done through business writing. Business writing is about facts – requesting or supplying. How you write will tell the reader about you, as the writer, the company (yours or whom you represent) and the image it generates of both.

Writing letters
Ask yourself 'Can the reader identify with what the letter is about?'

The heading
If possible, always include a heading leading into the main body of the letter. It lets the reader know instantly what the document is about.

Opening text
The opening sentence should try to sum up the main purpose of the letter from the reader's point of view.

Writing paragraphs
Each paragraph should deal with a new topic. Start your paragraph with its key sentence. Aim for variety in paragraph length. Stick to plain English using words that are familiar to your reader.

BUILDING YOUR NETWORK

If you have a particular problem at work, you might consider who else has already dealt with similar problems in your company (or out of it). You could network with your opposite numbers in similar organisations. Build up a contact list of work colleagues both inside and outside your company, external advisers and professional organisations.

CASE STUDIES

Carol wants to be a portfolio person
Carol is using her husband and her course tutor to build bridges into companies which offer jobshare vacancies in information technology. Carol wants a part-time job with a company while also working from home developing her own business as a conference organiser.

John is moving on up
John has enrolled on a Certificate in Management Studies. He intends writing speculative letters to get a job in betting shop management. He feels much more optimistic and motivated by this change in direction.

Iris is casting her net wider
Iris has begun her counselling diploma and is finding that her learning is opening her up to other possibilities in her work. She is casting her networking net wider to look for opportunities in management training, career counselling and stress-related counselling.

DISCUSSION POINTS

1. How does your gender network in your company?

2. What helps to keep the 'old boy network' in place?

3. How can mentoring help you step into management?

10
Cultivating for the Future

During the time you have been reading this book, we have been networking. I have information, knowledge and skills which I have put into a written format. You had a need, responded to the title of *Career Networking*, bought the book and read it. You would have known some of the content already, other parts would be new to you, some things you might disagree with, others you might try before making a decision.

UNDERSTANDING NETWORKING

Career networking brings people together. It builds bridges between what we each know and can share with each other. It is about making contact in order to exchange information.

Developing the confidence to network

In order to network, we need to feel confident in our skills and our methods of communication. If we don't think positively of ourselves, how can we market a confident self-image? Self-doubt can be helped by developing assertiveness. It doesn't come easy to many people to think well of themselves and to project their skills and strengths in a positive way. It isn't arrogant to believe in yourself. It would be arrogant if you believed that you possessed skills and strengths that you didn't have, especially if you put down other people in order to feel stronger yourself. Putting yourself down doesn't serve any purpose – it helps no one.

REMEMBERING THE KEY POINTS

As career networking is about information, it is important at this stage to re-affirm the key points of this book.

Being seen as a specialist

To have a single skill, especially a manual one, is no longer enough.

You need to be multiskilled and able to transfer your skills across occupations.

Improving your people skills
Career networking exists through effective communication. We need to build up our interpersonal skills not only for getting work but also to stay in work. We need to refine our communication skills to include informing, listening, supporting, guiding, making requests and showing appreciation.

Gathering information
In order to gain the maximum out of our career networking, we need to begin by establishing objectives and then identifying sources of information and ways to gather that information

Networking for the new workplace
The workplace of today is fast, streamlined and competitive. The companies you work for are facing tougher opposition than ever before. They have to cut back their overheads to stay in front. The permanent workforce is shrinking, giving way to part-time, temporary and contract workers who are flexible. As a worker, you are in competition with other workers. You need to run your working life like a business, identifying and increasing new ways to exploit your skills and knowledge and gaining visibility to potential employers.

Getting yourself noticed
Another facet of networking is to use technology, such as the Internet and fax. Getting your face known and gaining visibility as an expert may be helped through off-beat methods such as writing, holding a seminar, issuing a press release or creating a pressure group.

Networking while unemployed
If you are out of work, this can produce special types of problems. Motivation may be low and apathy high. As you withdraw from the mainstream of working life, your contacts shrink and you may experience isolation. If you are about to be (or have just been) made redundant, network before you leave or start up a redundancy network. If you are not working, use the Jobcentre, employment agencies, the library and your social circle to get job leads.

Networking in work
You may want to network at work for promotion, a sideways move

or to improve your skills base. Use presentations, meetings and conferences to raise your profile. Show yourself as a team member. Become more actively involved in your appraisal. Improve your business writing so that it becomes powerspeak.

Returning to study
You might be considering returning to training and education. Your Jobcentre will be able to give advice on free courses if you are unemployed. Your local library may have a TAPS (Training and Access Point) which can provide information on courses. Write to, telephone or visit colleges and universities.

EXTENDING YOUR NETWORK

Career networking is an infinite exercise. There is no end. You build up your contacts. Some will have a limited life-span and you will need to be constantly extending and rebuilding your links.

Starting your own network
You might choose to start your own network. Consider:

- a redundancy network

- a professional women's network

- a particular trade/profession network made up of local members

- a mentoring network.

Initial publicity could go through your local TEC, Chamber of Commerce or Enterprise Agency. You might have a newsletter, training days or monthly meetings.

Getting on other people's network
Another approach is to contact your local library, TEC or Chamber of Commerce and see if you can join a local group or association. At the time of writing this book, I belong to the Institute of Personnel and Development, Institute of Career Guidance, Business and Professional Women UK Ltd and the Society of Authors. All of these associations send me reading material, some have vacancies, all of them keep me informed of current trends and some give me business ideas.

BUILDING YOUR PERSONAL NETWORKING WEB

True networking covers the whole of your life, work, play, family and spiritual. Take time to look at the rest of your life.

Your domestic network
Who do you turn to when things go wrong or need doing around the home or in the garden?

Your health network
Who forms your basic health network? Do you have alternative therapists you can turn to?

Your transport network
Do you have the phone numbers of public transport contacts? Who do you turn to when something goes wrong with your car?

Your family network
Who do you turn to for baby-sitting or child-minding? Is there a network in place for dependants or ageing parents?

Your social network
Who do you socialise with on your own? Who do you meet with your partner? Do you know your partner's network of social contacts?

Your interest and hobby network
Do you network with specialist groups? Do you network through a magazine?

Your educational network
How do your educational needs get met? Do you have college or university contacts? Do you study at home?

Your personal support network
As well as your network of professional contacts, it is important to have a support network of people you can turn to for personal support. Ask yourself the following questions:

- Who can I rely upon in a crisis?
- Who can I talk to when I am worried?
- Who mentally stimulates me?

- Who can I have fun with socially?

- Who can I feel close to?

- Who values me?

- Who challenges me?

- Who gives me constructive feedback?

Your spiritual network
Who helps to guide and focus your spiritual needs?

BEING PART OF SOMEONE ELSE'S NETWORK

Your usefulness to others could link you to those people and place you in a position of power. Consider:

- In what ways could I mentor (act as a guide) or provide a role model for others?

- What useful skills might I use to be of benefit to others?

- How can I challenge others to bring out their best?

- What kind of people do I attract and why?

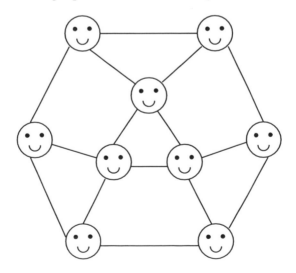

Fig. 22. Multiplying your contacts.

MULTIPLYING YOUR CONTACTS

If we each know fifty people on a professional and personal basis and multiply each of those fifty people by the fifty people they know, the numbers grow ever larger (see Figure 22). A network is any amount of people making up any amount of groups. Each person you know brings you into their network until your network ties in with many other networks. John Naisbett, the networking expert, says he can reach anyone, anywhere in the world in two contacts! We make contact on a daily basis, with around 20 people. Try to increase that number.

> **Career networking is the buying and selling of information through your skills and contacts.**

Stepping stones

Networking is creating and using stepping stones. Two or three years ago, I wrote a speculative letter to a publisher offering an idea for a book. I received an author's agreement for that book. This book is my fourth for that same publisher. Part of the process of writing a book is proof-reading. I now know Bill who co-ordinates that part. I've picked his brains about other aspects of writing. Writing these books has led onto writing a series of articles for a national magazine. These four books and the fifth, soon to be written, have opened the doors to having a literary agent. So it goes on.

You meet someone at a party, they know a man who's looking for someone to run his office. Your friend contacts him, tells him how wonderful you are, you phone him up, go for the interview and get the job. You build up administration experience, leave his employment, set up your own secretarial bureau and have your old employer as your first client. My husband, who's a printer, was made redundant after fifteen years with the same firm. Word went out on the printing network. Within two days, he was headhunted and had a job. Six years later when he was ready to leave that company, he contacted a friend who was influential in the local print union, found there was a job going in his company, applied for it and has now settled in there quite happily.

Several years ago, a close friend of mine who worked for Employment Services told me about government training schemes which she thought I could do training for. She gave me some contact names. From that particular path of stepping stones, I've networked through several training agencies, built up a reputation as a career development trainer and started writing about career management.

Communication information

I'm not entirely happy about the word 'networking'. Although a friendly person, I tend to keep myself quite private. When I was researching the material for this book, networking originally seemed to suggest being pushy and aggressive, risking rejection and not being good enough. I now interpret networking as communicating, finding out and exchanging useful information. I can then use the information in whatever way I choose. When people network with me, I see this as an affirmation of my skills and knowledge and I do all I can to be of help.

Male and female differences

Networking is a natural activity for most women. They relate and touch-base more often than men do. Sometimes I think I have more of a male attitude towards networking. Men tend to communicate for a specific purpose while women communicate for more personal reasons.

FINAL WORDS

Career networking is set to grow. We need it to find work and we need it to do our work. This book has been my way of networking with you. I have reached out with words and you have reached out with curiosity. Now it's up to you to extend your networking web and create your working future. Good luck!

It's not just who you know but who knows you.

CASE STUDIES

Carol is setting her aims high

Carol has work three mornings a week with a local software company as an administrator and word processor operator. She is using her husband's contacts to build up a company specialising in organising conferences for the computer industry.

John is managing his future
John now works for a betting company managing a shop. He has long-term ideas of transferring his skills across to casino management.

Iris is stressed out
Iris is using her networking skills to build up a stress-counselling business for executives.

DISCUSSION POINTS

1. One of the first steps in career networking is identifying potential market need. How do your current skills match local employers' needs?

2. When you have identified local needs, what can you do to make your skills more saleable?

3. How are you going to sell your skills above and beyond that of your competitors?

Glossary

Alexander technique. A natural health therapy involving the process of psycho-physical re-education and eliminating unnecessary tension in the way we move, react and use our bodies.

Assessing. A term linked to NVQs. Workplace assessment is where a candidates taking an NVQ is observed doing the task involved in a job, thereby creating evidence for assessment leading to an NVQ.

Coaching. One-to-one training.

Corporate culture. The ethos and philosophy of a company.

Customer care. A term used to describe customer relations, complaint handling and responding to customer needs.

CV. Curriculum Vitae. Your work history.

Delegating. A term used in management. It refers to the handing out of tasks to other people.

Diversify. To have a nucleus of skills from which you might branch out in various directions.

Empower. A current business trend involving the facilitation of other people's awareness of themselves and their place within a company so that they might become more effective decision-makers and leaders.

Gender. A term used to describe male or female.

Hierarchy. An upward and downward, authoritarian style common in many companies.

In-house. Keeping it in the company.

IT. Information technology.

Job enlargement. A current working term used to describe a job made larger through absorbing other jobs which have been made redundant.

Linguistic and cultural skills. Skills necessary to communicate with other countries.

Literacy. Reading and writing skills.

Lower-skilled jobs. A term largely referring to manual work.

Market forces. International and national economic, sociological and political forces which affect commerce and industry.

Multi-skilled. We now need to have a wide range of skills in order to stay in work.

Non-verbal communication. Body language.

Numeracy. Understanding and working with figures.

NVQ. National Vocational Qualification. These are employer-led and created by the lead industries of each profession and trade. They come in five levels and are obtained through providing evidence and being observed doing the job. NVQs are directly related to the workplace and the tasks your job entails.

Objectives. What is the end result we desire?

Peer group. People of our own generation.

Performance appraisal. A monthly, quarterly or yearly meeting, sometimes involving a written report, which analyses a worker's performance.

Pro-active. Taking the initiative.

Role models. People who provide us with examples of how we should feel, think or behave.

Sensory system. Our five senses.

Siblings. Brothers and sisters.

Speculative. Taking a chance, *eg* making a telephone call or writing a letter to a company enquiring about work opportunities.

Spiritual network. The people we know who provide support in our moral, ethical or religious search.

T'ai Chi. A natural health therapy which increases mental and physical energy through systematic stress reduction involving the whole body.

Technology. Any equipment using electricity or batteries, *eg* a production line, computers, printing presses or calculators.

Verbal communication. The ways in which we speak and the types of words and phrases we might use.

Visual aids. Aids we might use to assist us when giving a presentation or training. They might include flip-charts, over-head projectors, hand-outs, slide projectors, white-boards or black-boards.

Work experience. A term usually related to taking a vocational qualification whereby the candidate or trainee has experience of working in a commercial or industrial environment during part of their study-time.

Useful Addresses

BENEFITS

Social Security phone line: 0800 666555. Free.

CAREER DEVELOPMENT

British Institute of Management, Small Firms Information Centre, Management House, Cottingham Road, Corby, Northamptonshire NN17 1TT. Tel: (01536) 204222.

Business and Professional Women UK, 23 Ansdell Street, Kensington, London W8 5BN. Tel: (0171) 938 1729.

Careers & Occupational Information Centre (COIC), PO Box 348, Bristol BS99 7FE.

Careers Office. (Look in your local *Yellow Pages*.)

European Commission, Recruitment, Appointments & Promotion Division, DGIX, Commission of the European Communities, 200 Rue de la Loi, B-1049, Brussels, Belgium.

Executive Service, Heatherside House, Park Street, Camberley, Surrey GU15 3NY. (A jobsearch agency if you earn more than £15,000 per annum.)

Jobsharers, 11a Croft Close, Elford, Staffordshire B79 9BU. Tel: (01827) 383502. (A national jobshare register.)

New Ways to Work, 309 Upper Street, London N1 0PD. Tel: (0171) 226 4026.

Skill, National Bureau for Students with Disabilities, 336 Brixton Road, London SW9 7AA. Tel: (0171) 274 0565. (Develops opportunities in further and higher education and employment for those with disabilities or learning difficulties.)

EXAMINING AND ACCREDITING BODIES

Business & Technology Education Council (BTEC), Central House, Upper Woburn Place, London WC1H 0HH. Tel: (0171) 413 8400.

(Information on BTEC courses.)

City & Guilds of London Institute, Marketing and PR Department, 326 City Road, London EC1V 2PT. Tel: (0171) 278 2468. (Information on C & G courses including NVQs.)

Examinations of the Pitman Examinations Institute, Catteshall Manor, Godalming, Surrey GU7 1UU. Tel: (01483) 415311.

London Chamber of Commerce and Industry Examinations Board, Marlowe House, Station Road, Sidcup, Kent DA15 7BJ. Tel: (0181) 302 0261. (Information on administration, management and business qualifications.)

National Council for Vocational Qualifications, 222 Euston Road, London NW1 2BZ. Tel: (0171) 387 9898. (Information on NVQs.)

RSA Examinations Board, Westwood Way, Coventry CV4 8HS. Tel: (01203) 470033.

Scottish Vocational Education Council (SCOTVEC), Hanover House, 24 Douglas Street, Glasgow G2 7NQ. Tel: (0141) 248 7900. (Information on qualifications.)

SELF-EMPLOYMENT

British Franchise Association, Thames View, New Town Road, Henley-on-Thames, Oxon RG9 1HG. Tel: (01491) 578049.

Company Registration Office, Companies House, 55 City Road, London EC1Y 1BB. Tel: (0171) 253 9393.

DSS Office. (Look in your local *Yellow Pages*.)

Inland Revenue. (Look in your local *Yellow Pages*.)

National Federation of Self-Employed and Small Businesses Ltd, 32 St Anne's Road West, Lytham St Anne's, Lancashire FY8 1NY. Tel: (01253) 720911.

Rural Development Commission, 141 Castle Street, Salisbury, Wiltshire SP1 3TP. Tel: (01622) 765222. (Grants.)

The Trade Marks Registry. Tel: (0171) 438 4700.

Venture Capital Association, 3 Catherine Place, London SW1E 6DX. Tel: (0171) 233 5212.

TRAINING AND EDUCATION

Career Development Loans, Freepost, PO Box 99, Sudbury, Suffolk CO10 6BR. Freephone: 0800 585505.

Department of Health, Student Grant Unit, Morcross, Blackpool FY5 3TA. Tel: (01253) 856123. (Grants for occupational therapy, physiotherapy, radiography, dentistry.)

ECCTIS 2000, Fulton House, Jessop Avenue, Cheltenham, Gloucestershire GL50 3SH. Tel: (01242) 518724. (Computer databases found in colleges, careers offices, adult guidance services and libraries giving information on around 100,000 courses in the UK.)

Educational Grants Advisory Service, Family Welfare Association, 501/505 Kingsland Road, London E8.

Educational Liaison Officer, Channel 4 Television, 60 Charlotte Street, London W1P 2AX. (Learning from home via the TV.)

Insight Information, BBC, Broadcasting House, London W1A 1AA. (Learning from home via the TV.)

International Training and Recruitment Link, 56 High Street, Harston, Cambridge CB2 5PZ. Tel: (01223) 872747.

Jobcentres. (Look in your local *Yellow Pages.*)

Local Education Authorities (LEAs). (Look in your local *Yellow Pages*. Mandatory and discretionary grants.)

National Association for the Care and Resettlement of Offenders (NACRO), National Education Advisory Service, 567a Barlow Moor Road, Manchester M21 2AE. (Information and advice on colleges, courses and grants.)

National Council for Vocational Qualifications, 22 Euston Road, London NW1 2BZ. Tel: (0171) 728 1893.

National Extension College, 18 Brooklands Avenue, Cambridge CB2 2HN. Tel: (01223) 316644. (Study skills, GCSEs, A Levels, degrees, professional studies and languages.)

The Open College, St Paul's, 781 Wilmslow Road, Didsbury, Manchester M20 8RW. Tel: (0161) 434 0007. (Work-related courses including work skills, management and supervision, accountancy, health and care, technology and education and training.)

Open College of the Arts, Houndhill, Worsborough, Barnsley, South Yorkshire S70 6TU. Tle: (01891) 168902. (Art and design, creative writing, drawing, garden design, music, painting, photography, sculpture and textiles.)

The Open University, PO Box 71, Milton Keynes, MK7 6AG.

Project 2000. (Contact your local health authority. Bursaries for nursing.)

Radio Publicity, BBC, Broadcasting House, London W1A 1AA. Tel: (0171) 580 4468. (Learning from home via the radio.)

TECs. (Look in your local *Yellow Pages.*)

Training Access Points (TAPS), St Mary's House, c/o Moorfoot, Sheffield, South Yorkshire S1 4PQ.

Further Reading

BUSINESS PHILOSOPHY

Jobshift, William Bridges (Nicholas Brealey, 1995).
The Age of Unreason, Charles Handy (Arrow, 1995).

GENERAL CAREERS INFORMATION

Handbook of Free Careers Information in the UK (Trotman, 1993).
Occupations 96 (Careers and Occupation Information, PO Box 348, Bristol BS99 7FE. Tel: (0117) 9777199. Wide range of publications and booklets on career options.)

QUALIFICATIONS

British Qualifications (Kogan Page, 1994).
British Vocational Qualifications (Kogan Page, 1995).

CAREER DEVELOPMENT

Career Planning for Women, Laurel Alexander (How To Books, 1996).
Changing your Job after 35, Godfrey Golzen (Kogan Page, 1993).
Finding a Job with a Future, Laurel Alexander (How To Books, 1996).
Guidelines for the Redundant Manager (British Institute of Management).
How to Return to Work, Ann Dobson (How To Books, 1995).
How to Start a New Career, Judith Johnstone (How To Books, 2nd edition, 1994).
Job Ideas (COIC).
Job Search Guide, CEPEC Ltd, Princes House, 36 Jermyn Street, London SW1Y 6DN. (For executives and professionals.)
Jobs for the Over 50s. Linda Greenbury (Piatkus, 1994).
Just the Job, John Best (Nicholas Brealey, 1994).

Learning New Job Skills, Laurel Alexander (How To Books, 1997).
Offbeat Careers, Vivien Donald (Kogan Page, 1995).
Surviving Redundancy, Laurel Alexander (How To Books, 1996).
Your Services are No Longer Required, Christopher Kirkwood (Penguin, 1993).

DIRECTORIES

Directory of Directors.
Director of Grant Making Trusts. (List of funds available for research, education and training.)
Kelly's Business Directory. (Information on over 82,000 industrial, commercial and professional organisations in the UK.)
Times 1000 List of Companies. (Background information on major companies and establishments offering management and other training courses.)
Who Owns Whom. (Lists parent companies, their subsidiaries and associates.)

FUNDING

Department for Education and Employment, Publications Centre, PO Box 2193, London E15 2EU. (Tel: (0181) 533 2000. (Information on grants.)
MRC, Project Grants, 20 Park Crescent, London W1N 4AL. (Research and Training Opportunities and Project Grants.)
Sponsorships 1995, COIC, Department CW, ISCO5, The Paddock, Frizinghall, Bradford BD9 4HD.
Student Loan Company Ltd, 100 Bothwell Street, Glasgow G2 7GD. Tel: (0345) 300900. (Booklet on loans to students.)
Tax Relief for Vocational Training, Personal Taxpayers Leaflet IR 119 (Inland Revenue).
The Grant Register (Macmillan Press).

NEW WAYS OF WORKING

Directory of Jobs & Careers Abroad, Alex Lipinski (Vacation Work).
Guide to Working Abroad, Godfrey Golzen (*Daily Telegraph*/Kogan Page, 1994).
How to Get a Job Abroad, Roger Jones (How To Books, 4th edition, 1996).

How to Work From Home, Ian Phillipson (How To Books, 2nd edition, 1995).
Job Sharing: A Practical Guide, Pam Walton (Kogan Page, 1990).
National Council for One Parent Families, 255 Kentish Town Road, London NW5 2LX. Tel: (0171) 267 1361. (A guide is available helping in various ways.)
Working for Yourself, Godfrey Golzen (*Daily Telegraph*/Kogan Page, 1989).

SELLING YOURSELF

Body Language, Allan Pease (Sheldon Press, 1988).
CVs and Written Applications, Judy Skeats (Wardlock, 1987).
Effective Networking, Venda Raye-Johnson (Crisp Publications).
Effective Presentation, Anthony Jay (Pitman Publishing, 1994).
How to Write a CV That Works, Paul McGee (How To Books, 1995).
Presenting Yourself: A Personal Image Guide for Men, Mary Spillane (Piatkus).
Presenting Yourself: A Personal Image Guide for Women, Mary Spillane (Piatkus, 1993).
Winning Presentations, Ghassan Hasbani (How To Books, 1996).

POSITIVE THINKING

Effective Thinking Skills, Richard Nelson-Jones (Cassell, 1989).
Feel the Fear and Do It Anyway, Susan Jeffers (Arrow, 1987).

TRAINING AND EDUCATION

British Qualifications (Kogan Page, 1994). (A guide to educational, technical, professional and academic qualifications in Britain.)
British Vocational Qualifications (Kogan Page, 1995). (A directory of vocational qualifications available from all awarding bodies in Britain.)
Degree Course Guides (CRAC, Hobsons Press, bi-annually).
Directory of Further Education, The Comprehensive Guide to Courses in UK Polytechnics and Colleges, James Tomlinson and David Weighall (CRAC, Hobsons Press, annually).
How to Study and Learn, Peter Marshall (How To Books, 1995).
How to Study Effectively, Richard Freeman and John Meed (National Extension College, 1993).

Second Chances: Guide to Adult Education and Training Opportunities (COIC, 1993).

Unemployment and Training Rights Handbook (Unemployment Unit, 409 Briston Road, London SW9 7DG).

Index

PASSING THAT INTERVIEW
Your step-by-step guide to achieving success

Judith Johnstone

Everyone knows how to shine at interview – or do they? When every candidate becomes the perfect clone of the one before, you have to have that extra 'something' to raise your chances above the rest. Using a systematic and practical approach, this How To book takes you step-by-step through the essential pre-interview groundwork, the interview encounter itself, and what you can learn from the experience afterwards. The book contains sample pre- and post-interview correspondence, and is complete with a guide to further reading, glossary of terms, and index. 'This is from the first class How To Books stable.' *Escape Committee Newsletter.* 'Offers a fresh approach to a well documented subject.' *Newscheck/Careers Service Bulletin.* 'A complete step-by-step guide.' *The Association of Business Executives.* Judith Johnstone is a Graduate of the Institute of Personnel & Development; she has been an instructor in Business Studies and adult literacy tutor, and has long experience of helping people at work.

144pp. illus. 1 85703 360 4. 4th edition.

CAREER PLANNING FOR WOMEN
How to make a positive impact on your working life

Laurel Alexander

More women are entering the workplace than ever before. Whether it is on the corporate ladder or self employed, women are establishing a much stronger place for themselves within the world of commerce and industry. As global and national markets shift and business ethos develops, the specific qualities of women play a vital part alongside those of men. Business has been influenced primarily by male thought and action. Now there is the opportunity for women to make a substantial contribution with new ideas and approaches. The book is not about women taking men's jobs or about women being better or worse than men. It is intended to help women understand their unique and emerging role in business, change their perception of themselves and take much more responsibility for their responses and actions within the workplace. Laurel Alexander is a manager/trainer in career development who has helped many individuals succeed in changing their work direction. She is also author of *Surviving Redundancy* in this series.

160pp. illus. 1 85703 417 1.

How To Books

How To Books provide practical help on a large range of topics. They are available through all good bookshops or can be ordered direct from the distributors. Just tick the titles you want and complete the form on the following page.

___ Apply to an Industrial Tribunal (£7.99)
___ Applying for a Job (£8.99)
___ Applying for a United States Visa (£15.99)
___ Backpacking Round Europe (£8.99)
___ Be a Freelance Journalist (£8.99)
___ Be a Freelance Secretary (£8.99)
___ Become a Freelance Sales Agent (£9.99)
___ Become an Au Pair (£8.99)
___ Becoming a Father (£8.99)
___ Buy & Run a Shop (£8.99)
___ Buy & Run a Small Hotel (£8.99)
___ Buying a Personal Computer (£9.99)
___ Career Networking (£8.99)
___ Career Planning for Women (£8.99)
___ Cash from your Computer (£9.99)
___ Choosing a Nursing Home (£9.99)
___ Choosing a Package Holiday (£8.99)
___ Claim State Benefits (£9.99)
___ Collecting a Debt (£9.99)
___ Communicate at Work (£7.99)
___ Conduct Staff Appraisals (£7.99)
___ Conducting Effective Interviews (£8.99)
___ Coping with Self Assessment (£9.99)
___ Copyright & Law for Writers (£8.99)
___ Counsel People at Work (£7.99)
___ Creating a Twist in the Tale (£8.99)
___ Creative Writing (£9.99)
___ Critical Thinking for Students (£8.99)
___ Dealing with a Death in the Family (£9.99)
___ Do Voluntary Work Abroad (£8.99)
___ Do Your Own Advertising (£8.99)
___ Do Your Own PR (£8.99)
___ Doing Business Abroad (£10.99)
___ Doing Business on the Internet (£12.99)
___ Emigrate (£9.99)
___ Employ & Manage Staff (£8.99)
___ Find Temporary Work Abroad (£8.99)
___ Finding a Job in Canada (£9.99)
___ Finding a Job in Computers (£8.99)
___ Finding a Job in New Zealand (£9.99)
___ Finding a Job with a Future (£8.99)
___ Finding Work Overseas (£9.99)
___ Freelance DJ-ing (£8.99)
___ Freelance Teaching & Tutoring (£9.99)
___ Get a Job Abroad (£10.99)
___ Get a Job in America (£9.99)
___ Get a Job in Australia (£9.99)
___ Get a Job in Europe (£9.99)
___ Get a Job in France (£9.99)
___ Get a Job in Travel & Tourism (£8.99)
___ Get into Radio (£8.99)
___ Getting into Films & Television (£10.99)

___ Getting That Job (£8.99)
___ Getting your First Job (£8.99)
___ Going to University (£8.99)
___ Helping your Child to Read (£8.99)
___ How to Study & Learn (£8.99)
___ Investing in People (£9.99)
___ Investing in Stocks & Shares (£9.99)
___ Keep Business Accounts (£7.99)
___ Know Your Rights at Work (£8.99)
___ Live & Work in America (£9.99)
___ Live & Work in Australia (£12.99)
___ Live & Work in Germany (£9.99)
___ Live & Work in Greece (£9.99)
___ Live & Work in Italy (£8.99)
___ Live & Work in New Zealand (£9.99)
___ Live & Work in Portugal (£9.99)
___ Live & Work in the Gulf (£9.99)
___ Living & Working in Britain (£8.99)
___ Living & Working in China (£9.99)
___ Living & Working in Hong Kong (£10.99)
___ Living & Working in Israel (£10.99)
___ Living & Working in Saudi Arabia (£12.99)
___ Living & Working in the Netherlands (£9.99)
___ Making a Complaint (£8.99)
___ Making a Wedding Speech (£8.99)
___ Manage a Sales Team (£8.99)
___ Manage an Office (£8.99)
___ Manage Computers at Work (£8.99)
___ Manage People at Work (£8.99)
___ Manage Your Career (£8.99)
___ Managing Budgets & Cash Flows (£9.99)
___ Managing Meetings (£8.99)
___ Managing Your Personal Finances (£8.99)
___ Managing Yourself (£8.99)
___ Market Yourself (£8.99)
___ Master Book-Keeping (£8.99)
___ Mastering Business English (£8.99)
___ Master GCSE Accounts (£8.99)
___ Master Public Speaking (£8.99)
___ Migrating to Canada (£12.99)
___ Obtaining Visas & Work Permits (£9.99)
___ Organising Effective Training (£9.99)
___ Pass Exams Without Anxiety (£7.99)
___ Passing That Interview (£8.99)
___ Plan a Wedding (£7.99)
___ Planning Your Gap Year (£8.99)
___ Prepare a Business Plan (£8.99)
___ Publish a Book (£9.99)
___ Publish a Newsletter (£9.99)
___ Raise Funds & Sponsorship (£7.99)
___ Rent & Buy Property in France (£9.99)
___ Rent & Buy Property in Italy (£9.99)

___ Research Methods (£8.99)	___ Use the Internet (£9.99)
___ Retire Abroad (£8.99)	___ Winning Consumer Competitions (£8.99)
___ Return to Work (£7.99)	___ Winning Presentations (£8.99)
___ Run a Voluntary Group (£8.99)	___ Work from Home (£8.99)
___ Setting up Home in Florida (£9.99)	___ Work in an Office (£7.99)
___ Spending a Year Abroad (£8.99)	___ Work in Retail (£8.99)
___ Start a Business from Home (£7.99)	___ Work with Dogs (£8.99)
___ Start a New Career (£6.99)	___ Working Abroad (£14.99)
___ Starting to Manage (£8.99)	___ Working as a Holiday Rep (£9.99)
___ Starting to Write (£8.99)	___ Working in Japan (£10.99)
___ Start Word Processing (£8.99)	___ Working in Photography (£8.99)
___ Start Your Own Business (£8.99)	___ Working in the Gulf (£10.99)
___ Study Abroad (£8.99)	___ Working in Hotels & Catering (£9.99)
___ Study & Live in Britain (£7.99)	___ Working on Contract Worldwide (£9.99)
___ Studying at University (£8.99)	___ Working on Cruise Ships (£9.99)
___ Studying for a Degree (£8.99)	___ Write a Press Release (£9.99)
___ Successful Grandparenting (£8.99)	___ Write a Report (£8.99)
___ Successful Mail Order Marketing (£9.99)	___ Write an Assignment (£8.99)
___ Successful Single Parenting (£8.99)	___ Write & Sell Computer Software (£9.99)
___ Survive Divorce (£8.99)	___ Write for Publication (£8.99)
___ Surviving Redundancy (£8.99)	___ Write for Television (£8.99)
___ Taking in Students (£8.99)	___ Writing a CV that Works (£8.99)
___ Taking on Staff (£8.99)	___ Writing a Non Fiction Book (£9.99)
___ Taking Your A-Levels (£8.99)	___ Writing an Essay (£8.99)
___ Teach Abroad (£8.99)	___ Writing & Publishing Poetry (£9.99)
___ Teach Adults (£8.99)	___ Writing & Selling a Novel (£8.99)
___ Teaching Someone to Drive (£8.99)	___ Writing Business Letters (£8.99)
___ Travel Round the World (£8.99)	___ Writing Reviews (£9.99)
___ Understand Finance at Work (£8.99)	___ Writing Your Dissertation (£8.99)
___ Use a Library (£7.99)	

To: Plymbridge Distributors Ltd, Plymbridge House, Estover Road, Plymouth PL6 7PZ. Customer Services Tel: (01752) 202301. Fax: (01752) 202331.

Please send me copies of the titles I have indicated. Please add postage & packing (UK £1, Europe including Eire, £2, World £3 airmail).

☐ I enclose cheque/PO payable to Plymbridge Distributors Ltd for £ ☐

☐ Please charge to my ☐ MasterCard, ☐ Visa, ☐ AMEX card.

Account No. ☐☐☐☐☐☐☐☐☐☐☐☐☐☐☐☐

Card Expiry Date ☐ ☐ 19 ☎ **Credit Card orders may be faxed or phoned.**

Customer Name (CAPITALS) ....

Address ....

.... Postcode ....

Telephone .... Signature ....

Every effort will be made to despatch your copy as soon as possible but to avoid possible disappointment please allow up to 21 days for despatch time (42 days if overseas). Prices and availability are subject to change without notice.

Code BPA